This book belongs to:

....

Mrs Wordsmith®

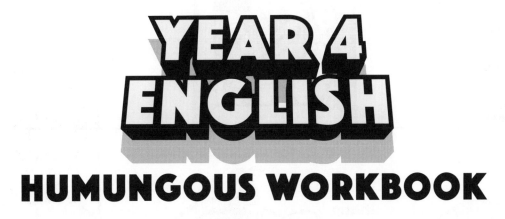

YEAR 4 ENGLISH

HUMUNGOUS WORKBOOK

MEET THE
CHARACTERS

Yang

Bogart

Oz

Yin

Armie

Bearnice

Shang
High

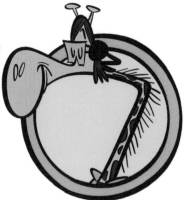

Brick

Grit

Plato

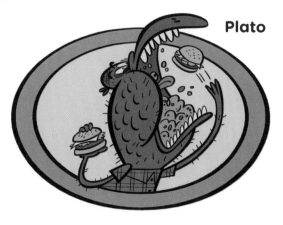

CONTENTS

Welcome to the Year 4 Humungous Workbook!

What's inside?

In this book, you will find everything you need to whizz through English in Year 4. It is divided into five chapters: **Grammar**, **Punctuation**, **Vocabulary**, **Spelling** and **Reading and Writing**. Each chapter combines targeted teaching of key skills, illustrations and activities. It's perfect for those learning something for the first time and for those who are just revising!

How do I use it?

However you want to! Start in the middle, start at the end or you could even start at the beginning if you're feeling traditional. Take it slowly and do one section at a time, or charge through the pages like a cheetah on the loose! Don't worry if something is too difficult. You'll get there in the end and there are tips and reminders to help you along the way.

Look out for this icon at the beginning of a new topic. It tells you that there's some important learning to do before you start answering the questions!

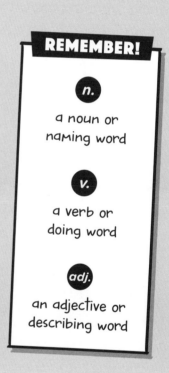

REMEMBER!

n.

a noun or naming word

v.

a verb or doing word

adj.

an adjective or describing word

How do I check my answers?

There's an answer key at the back! Checking answers is an important part of learning. Take care to notice and remember the ones you didn't know.

Oh, and please excuse Mrs Wordsmith's cast of out-of-control animals. They pop up all over the place and are usually up to no good.

Now, go and have some fun! And who knows, you might learn something along the way.

GRAMMAR

Grammar teaches you how to use different kinds of words (like verbs, nouns or adjectives) in all of their forms and to make different kinds of sentences in the past, present or future tense. When you master basic grammar rules, you have the power to talk or write about anything. When you master some more advanced grammar rules, you have the power to write beautifully.

A noun is the name of a **person**
or **animal**, **place** or **thing**.

Common nouns name general places or things.

cactus   sofa   cow

Proper nouns name specific people,
places or things. These always begin
with a capital letter.

Thursday   Jamaica   Bearnice

1 **Circle the common nouns and underline the proper nouns in these sentences.**

a. The television had been on for ten days.

b. The girl dreamed of visiting Morocco.

c. On Saturday, Armie went to the library.

d. The dog had last been spotted in Brazil.

e. The food in Tokyo was absolutely delicious.

f. The sculpture really inspired Plato.

2 **Now it's your turn!**
Write down three common nouns and three proper nouns.

Common nouns: ....

Proper nouns: ....

A **phrase** is a group of words without a main verb.

A **noun phrase** is a group of words that tells you about a noun.

Noun phrases can come in different lengths and styles, but they always add extra information about the noun.

an old **wizard**

an old **wizard**
with a white beard

1 Rewrite these nouns as descriptive noun phrases.
The first one is done for you.

a. cats — the hungry cats in the garden

b. kangaroo

c. actor

d. mountain

e. bacteria

f. asteroid

g. piano

h. shampoo

i. castle

Pronouns are short words that can take the place of **nouns** in a sentence. Without pronouns, sentences can get repetitive very quickly.

Shang High has been to the cinema five times this week because Shang High loves films.

Shang High's name was mentioned twice in that sentence. It's important to use Shang High's name the first time to introduce who the story is about. After that, his name can be replaced with a pronoun. These types of pronouns are called **subject pronouns**. They replace the noun that acts as the subject (the noun performing the action) in the sentence.

Shang High has been to the cinema five times this week because **he** loves films.

This makes the sentence less repetitive and easier to read!

Subject pronoun	Who or what the pronoun refers to
I	yourself (the one reading this workbook!)
you	a person or group that you (the reader) are addressing
he	a male person
she	a female person
it	an object or thing
we	more than one person, including you (the reader)
they	more than one person, not including you (the reader) **or** a person whose gender you don't know **or** a person who does not identify as male or female

1 **Rewrite these sentences and replace the nouns in bold with a suitable subject pronoun.**

Use the table on the opposite page to help you.

a. Brick was ravenous so **Brick** demolished

his lunch in thirty seconds.

....

....

....

b. Yin and Yang laughed joyfully as **Yin and Yang** leaped up and down.

....

....

2 **Improve the story below by adding subject pronouns.**

This story is too repetitive! First, read it and then write a suitable subject pronoun above the underlined nouns. The first one has been done for you.

she

Oz took a deep bow when Oz finished the performance.

The performance had been a huge success and the crowd went

wild. Oz looked out at the audience and smiled when she saw

Brick because Brick was jumping up and down and clapping.

Oz skipped off stage with a huge smile on her face. Oz couldn't

wait to go and meet her friends because her friends had promised

Oz a big celebration.

Remember, **pronouns** are short words that can take the place of **nouns** in a sentence. Without pronouns, sentences can get repetitive very quickly.

We have just learned about **subject pronouns**. These replace the noun that acts as the subject (the noun performing the action) in the sentence.

Brick loved sport so **Brick** played tennis.  Brick loved sport so **he** played tennis.

Object pronouns replace nouns that act as the object (the noun that the action is done to) in the sentence.

Bearnice challenged **Brick** to a race. → Bearnice challenged **him** to a race.

Some object pronouns look a little different to subject pronouns.

Object pronoun	Who or what the pronoun refers to
me	yourself (the one reading this workbook!)
you	a person or group that you (the reader) are addressing
him	a male person
her	a female person
it	an object or thing
us	more than one person, including you (the reader)
them	more than one person, not including you (the reader) **or** a person whose gender you don't know **or** a person who does not identify as male or female

1 **Complete the diary entry using the object pronouns below.**
Use each pronoun once.

us	it	her	them

Dear Diary,

Bearnice is one of my best friends. Yesterday, I invited Bearnice

to the beach. We had the best time! I bought an ice cream

and ate the ice cream by the water. Yum! There were lots of

seagulls and we filmed the seagulls stealing people's chips.

Then we went paddling in the sea and a big wave almost

knocked me and Bearnice over! It was amazing.

2 **Edit these sentences and replace the nouns in bold with a suitable object pronoun.**
Use the table on the opposite page to help you.

a. Bogart pranked **Yin and Yang**.

b. Oz texted **Brick**.

c. Grit pushed **Oz**.

d. Bearnice hugged **the teddy bear**.

e. Armie found **me and Grit** up a tree.

Remember, **pronouns** are short words that can take the place of **nouns** in a sentence.

Possessive pronouns show who owns something.

She has a ticket.

The ticket is **hers**.

"hers" is a possessive pronoun used instead of the noun phrase "her ticket"

Possessive pronoun	Who or what the pronoun refers to
mine	yourself (the one reading this workbook!)
yours	a person or group that you (the reader) are addressing
his	a male person
hers	a female person
its	an object or thing
ours	more than one person, including you (the reader)
theirs	more than one person, not including you (the reader) **or** a person whose gender you don't know **or** a person who does not identify as male or female

1 **Rewrite these sentences with possessive pronouns.**
The first one has been done for you.

a. That is **my apple**.   →   That apple is mine.

b. That is **Grit's ball**.   →   ....

c. Those are **Yin and**   →   ....

Yang's socks.   ....

d. That is **your hat**. → ....

e. That is **Oz's shoe**. → ....

f. Those are **mine and** → ....

Brick's seats. ....

2 Circle the correct pronoun to complete these sentences.

Watch out! This activity mixes subject, object and possessive pronouns. Think about what sounds right when you read these sentences aloud.

a. Armie was late to class but

(he) (him) desperately needed

to use the bathroom.

b. "What are you doing, Oz? That wallet is

(me) (mine) !" cried Brick.

c. Bearnice was drooling by the time the

waiter brought **she** **her** some food.

A **relative clause** can be used to give additional information about a noun.

noun

The <u>car</u>, **which was full of balloons**, slowly lifted off the ground.

relative clause

Relative clauses are separated from the rest of the sentence by commas. If the relative clause is in the middle of the sentence, then you need a comma before and after it, like:

relative clause

My sister, **who is three years older than me**, gave me a present.

comma

comma

If the relative clause is at the end of the sentence, then you only need a comma before it, like:

relative clause   *comma*   *full stop*

It's nearly summer,
which is my favourite time of year.

Relative clauses are introduced using a relative pronoun. We are going to focus on two of the most common relative pronouns: **who** and **which**.

Who is used to add extra information about a person or character, like:

The singer, **who** only sings in German, has a beautiful voice.

Which is used to add extra information about things, like:

The pizza, **which** was covered in nails, was inedible.

1 **Can you add the correct punctuation to these sentences with relative clauses?**

Remember, if the relative clause is in the middle of the sentence, it needs a comma before and after it. If the relative clause is at the end of the sentence, it needs a comma before it and a full stop after it.

a. The treasure chest which nobody had laid eyes on in 100 years was sticking out of the sand

b. Oz opened the door for Bearnice who had brought fifty cupcakes with her

c. The ancient tree which had been standing there for many centuries fell to the ground

d. Yin who had never used a VR headset before was completely immersed in the experience

2 **Add a relative clause to these sentences.**

Fill in the gaps with additional information. Remember to use **who** when you're talking about a person or character and **which** when you're talking about a thing.

a. Bearnice, ...
.... , was not impressed by the fireworks.

b. The telephone, ...
.... , stopped ringing.

c. Plato knocked on the door of the house, ...
....

d. The slime, ...
.... , had a horrible texture.

Verbs are **doing** and **being** words.

A **doing word** describes an action. For example, **play** is a doing word.

A **being word** describes a state of being. For example, **am** is a being word.

Tense tells us when something takes place. Things can happen in the past, present or future. When a sentence has more than one verb in it, they are usually in the same tense.

The **present tense** can be used to talk about something that **happens regularly**.

Bearnice **plays** chess.

TIP!

When the subject is singular, add –s to the present tense verb. When the subject is plural or the subject is I or you, do not add –s to the present tense verb.

The **past tense** can be used to talk about something that has **finished happening**. Remember, past tense verbs often end in -**ed**.

Bearnice **played** chess.

1 Rewrite these verbs in the past tense.

a. laugh ....

c. wander ....

b. stroll ....

d. crawl ....

2 Rewrite these verbs in the present tense.

a. I whispered ....

c. he stumbled ....

b. she sighed ....

d. you tiptoed ....

While regular past tense verbs end in **-ed**,
irregular past tense verbs are spelled and pronounced differently.
These are words you have to learn by heart, so let's get practising!

TIP!

It can be helpful to say the verbs aloud in a sentence,
like "Today, I sing" or "Yesterday, I sang".

1 Find the matching verbs.

Draw lines from the present tense verb to its matching irregular past
tense verb. It may look a little different, but read through all the answers
to work out which ones are pairs.

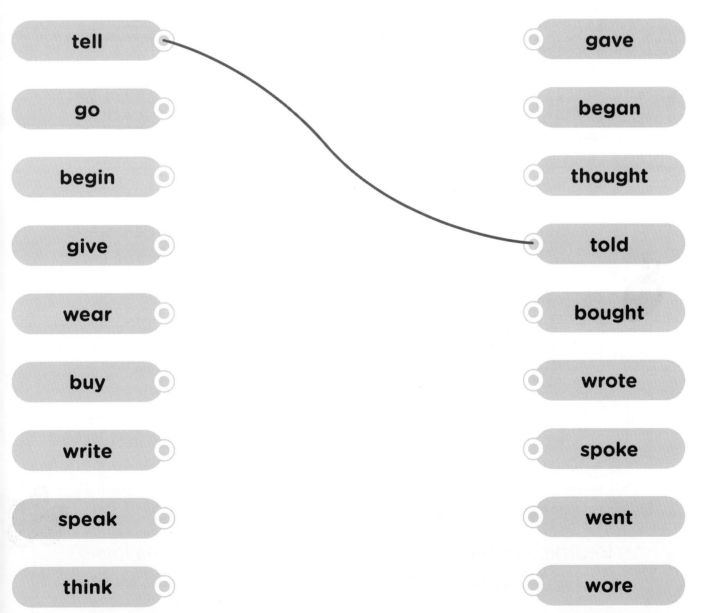

tell	gave
go	began
begin	thought
give	told
wear	bought
buy	wrote
write	spoke
speak	went
think	wore

Tense tells us when something takes place.
Things can happen in the past, present or future.

When a sentence has more than one verb in it,
they are usually in the **same tense**.

1 Complete these sentences.

Draw lines to match the two halves of the sentence together.
Use the tenses to help you.

a. Oz searches the whole house — and watches the sheep graze.

b. Grit walks through a field — after he bought a new cookbook.

c. Bearnice cried all night — and finds a secret clue.

d. Shang High loves strawberries — and hoped some flowers would grow.

e. Plato baked a chocolate cake — because she broke her favourite pencil.

f. Bearnice watered her garden — but he loves blueberries even more!

2 **Edit this text about Mount Vesuvius.**

The writer has made some mistakes in this story. They forgot to stay in the same tense. The underlined verbs are in the incorrect tense. Write your correction above each one. Some of them are irregular past tense verbs so make sure they sound right when you read them aloud.

Mount Vesuvius is an active volcano in southern Italy. Every year, 2.5 million people visit this famous volcano and <u>explored</u> the city of Pompeii below it.

Mount Vesuvius erupted in the year 79CE and lava, ash and mud <u>bury</u> the city of Pompeii. The city stayed buried until the 1700s, when archaeologists <u>begin</u> to dig up the ruins of the city. The archaeologists found that the volcanic ash <u>preserves</u> the city, meaning they could accurately see what life was like in the Roman Empire around 2,000 years ago. They even found graffiti written by the people who <u>live</u> in the town before the eruption.

For actions that are **still happening**, use the present form of **to be** and the main verb ending with -**ing**.

Bearnice **is skating**.

For actions that **were happening**, use the past form of **to be** and the main verb ending with -**ing**.

Bearnice **was skating**.

Remember, **to be** is an **irregular verb**.

Present tense	Past tense
I am	I was
you are	you were
he/she/it is	he/she/it was
we are	we were
you are	you were
they are	they were

---

1 **Rewrite the verbs in these phrases so that they are still happening.**

Remember to use the present form of **to be** and add -**ing** to the main verb.

a. Bearnice speaks   →   ....

b. Yin and Yang bake   →   ....

c. you consider   →   ....

d. I sing   →   ....

2 **Rewrite the verbs in these phrases so that they were happening.**

Remember to use the past form of **to be** and add -**ing** to the main verb.

a. Brick and Bogart build   →   ....

b. I expect   →   ....

c. he observes   →   ....

d. we race   →   ....

The present form of **to have** can be used to describe something that happened recently. Usually, the main verb remains in the past tense.

"I **have worked** very hard on this prank," announced Bogart.

Remember, **to have** is an **irregular verb**.

Present tense
I have
you have
he/she/it has
we have
you have
they have

1 **Rewrite these sentences with the present form of to have.**
Remember to transform the main verb in bold into the past tense. Watch out for irregular past tense verbs!

a. Shang High and Oz **relax** all day.

....

b. Armie **reads** lots of adventure books.

....

c. They **carry** the heavy bags for you.

....

d. You **dance** the tango.

....

e. I **tell** funny stories.

....

Modal verbs are used to change the meaning of other verbs.

The main modal verbs are **will**, **would**, **can**, **could**, **may**, **might**, **shall**, **should**, **ought** and **must**. These can express degrees of possibility as well as permission or obligation.

Brick helped Armie. → Brick **might** help Armie.

Might is the modal verb here. It expresses the likelihood of Brick helping Armie. It means that it is not certain that Brick will help Armie, but there is a chance that he will.

Modal verb	How it's used	What it means
will (past tense: would)	She **will** sing later today.	It is certain that she will sing in the future.
can (past tense: could)	She **can** sing very well.	She has the ability to sing very well.
may (more formal than might)	She **may** sing later.	There is a chance she will sing in the future.
might (less formal than may)	She **might** sing later.	There is a chance she will sing in the future.
shall	She **shall** sing a beautiful song.	She intends to sing a song in the future.
should	She **should** sing now.	It is necessary for her to sing.
ought	She **ought** to sing now.	It is very necessary for her to sing.
must	She **must** sing now.	It is extremely necessary for her to sing.

1 **Underline the modal verbs in these sentences.**

a. The pirate must walk the plank.

b. Bearnice might forget your birthday.

c. Grit should fight the sea monster.

d. Oz can speak fourteen languages.

2 **Read the sentences and answer the questions.**

a. **Grit might sleep.**

Shang High will sleep.

Who is more likely to sleep?

....

b. **Brick ought to score a goal.**

Yang shall score a goal.

Who is more certain to score a goal?

....

c. **Oz must win the race.**

Bearnice should win the race.

Who needs to win the race the most?

....

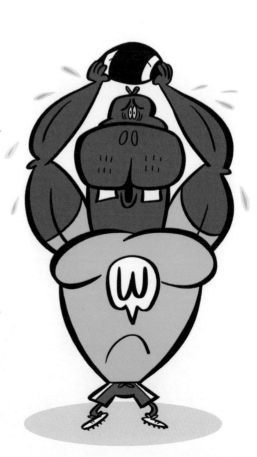

Let's look at some adjectives that describe scary things.

precipitous

adj. steep or dangerously high; like the edge of a very scary mountain

WORD PAIRS

precipitous **cliff**

precipitous **slope**

ominous

adj. scary, threatening or menacing; like a huge, dark tornado spinning in your direction

WORD PAIRS

ominous **clouds**

ominous **sign**

perilous

adj. risky or dangerous; like rafting through terrifying rapids

WORD PAIRS

perilous **water**

perilous **journey**

Adjectives are words that describe nouns.

sinister

adj. ominous, eerie or menacing; like mysterious lights in the middle of the night

--- WORD PAIRS ---

sinister **atmosphere**
sinister **behaviour**

deafening

adj. very noisy or thunderous; like an aeroplane landing behind you

--- WORD PAIRS ---

deafening **noise**
deafening **roar**

eerie

adj. weird, ghostly or creepy; like a spooky room full of skeletons and cobwebs

--- WORD PAIRS ---

eerie **silence**
eerie **music**

1 Complete these sentences.

Fill in the gaps with one of these adjectives or choose your own!

| perilous | eerie | precipitous | ominous | sinister | deafening |

a. The inside of the abandoned mansion was extremely

....

b. There was something .... about the

graveyard at night.

c. Oz peered over the cliff at the .... drop.

d. The sudden appearance of twenty crows was very

....

e. Shang High set off on a .... journey

through the jungle.

f. Armie's whole body shook when

he heard the ....

crash of the cymbals.

Adverbs describe **verbs**. Remember, a verb is a doing or being word. Adverbs often end in **-ly**. They describe how or when we do things.

Adverbs can often be made by adding **-ly** to adjectives:

precipitous ➕ ly ➖ **precipitously**

1 Complete these sentences.

Fill in the gaps with one of these adverbs or choose your own!
If you aren't sure what these adverbs mean, have a look at pages
28–29 and the adjectives that are defined there.

perilously   eerily   precipitously   ominously   sinisterly   deafeningly

a. The alarm clock made a .... loud noise.

b. The path winds .... up the mountain.

c. The wind howled .... through the trees.

d. Bogart smiled .... as he laid out his evil plan.

e. The lights flickered ....

f. Oz balanced ....

on the tightrope.

A phrase is a group of words without a verb. Some phrases behave like adverbs. **Adverbial phrases** describe how, when or where a verb happens.

I saw a giant goose **in the distance**.

When these adverbial sentences go at the start of a sentence and add extra information, they are called **fronted adverbials**. Remember, fronted adverbials are always followed by a comma that separates them from the rest of the sentence.

In the distance, I saw a giant goose.

1 **Circle the adverbial phrases.**

Does it describe how, when or where something happened?

after a while   far away   a horseshoe

by the bank of the river   a new invention   very bravely

2 **Underline the adverbial phrases in these sentences.**

Watch out! Not all sentences will have an adverbial phrase.

a. Bearnice opened the email as fast as she could.

b. Above the clouds, a giant plotted her revenge.

c. Shang High forgot his umbrella.

d. The magician vanished in the blink of an eye.

e. The waterfall cascaded over the edge of the cliff.

3 **Complete these sentences by adding the adverbial phrase.**

Don't forget to add capital letters to the start of sentences and commas to fronted adverbial phrases.

> **all of a sudden**

> **with an intense passion**

> **back at the train station**

a. .... the delays were causing crowds to gather.

b. .... the floodwater began to rise.

c. Shang High made music ....

4 **Write your own sentences with adverbial phrases.**

Base your sentences on the images and try to write one sentence with a fronted adverbial.

a. ....

....

....

....

b. ....

....

....

....

Most sentences are made up of **clauses**. A clause contains a **verb**.

A **main clause** forms a complete sentence on its own. This means that it doesn't need any extra information to make sense.

Brick counted sheep.

A **subordinate clause** does not make sense on its own. It adds extra information to the main clause and it contains a subordinating conjunction, such as **because**, **after**, **when** or **until**.

Subordinate clauses can go at the beginning or the end of a sentence. When the subordinate clause is at the beginning, it is followed by a **comma**.

main clause
→ Brick counted sheep
until he fell asleep.
— subordinate clause

subordinate clause   comma
→ Until he fell asleep,
Brick counted sheep.
— main clause

① Underline the subordinate clause in each sentence.

a. Brick missed the goal because a fly flew into his mouth.

b. Yin gasped loudly when Yang told her the secret.

c. When Grit felt sad, he liked to go for a long walk.

② Underline the subordinating conjunction and add commas where necessary.

Remember to watch out for subordinate clauses at the start of sentences.

a. After waiting hours for the lift Plato took the stairs.

b. Oz loves going to the dentist because she gets a sticker.

c. When it gets cold Bearnice wears gloves and a scarf.

3 Now it's your turn!

Complete these sentences by writing
your own subordinate clause in the gaps.

a. Grit thought he had caught a gigantic fish

....

....

b. Yin ate a decadent slice of chocolate

fudge cake ....

....

c. ....

.... ,

Bogart chuckled softly.

d. Yang confidently skied down the mountain

....

....

A preposition links a noun, pronoun or noun phrase to some other word in the sentence. Prepositions often tell us where something happens (place) or when something happens (time). Examples of prepositions include words like **in**, **on**, **after, before, under** and **outside**.

The party is **in** my house.

1 **Choose a preposition to complete the sentence and describe the image.**

under	on	next to

a. Shang High is sitting .... a pile of clothes.

b. The teddy bear is .... the carpet.

c. The toy car is .... the banana peel.

2 **Circle the most suitable preposition.**
Use the rest of the sentence as a clue.

a. Grit took a nap (**under**   **among**) the sink.

b. Yang celebrated (**after**   **before**) winning the race.

c. Armie sat (**beside**   **below**) Grit on the first day of school.

d. Shang High is so tall he can see (**above**   **during**) the clouds.

e. Bogart met Armie (**outside**   **between**) the library.

f. Plato loves tacos with cheese (**on**   **in**) top.

Simple sentences have one main clause and one idea.

Plato bought a burrito.

Compound sentences have at least two main clauses that are joined with a coordinating conjunction.

Main clause

coordinating conjunction

Plato bought a burrito **and**

he ate it in less than seven seconds.

Main clause

REMEMBER

Conjunctions are joining words that can connect clauses (parts of a sentence).

The most common conjunctions are **and**, **or** and **but**. They are used to join two main clauses together. They are called coordinating conjunctions.

REMEMBER!

A main clause can form a complete sentence on its own but it can also form part of a compound sentence.

① Circle the most suitable conjunction.

a. Yang wanted to be a secret agent **and** **but** she wanted to find out everyone's secrets.

b. Brick counted his toes every night **or** **and** he counted his fingers every morning.

c. Bogart wanted to take over the world **but** **or** Bearnice always stopped him.

d. Plato wanted to open a food truck **or** **but** he wanted to open a restaurant.

2 Complete these compound sentences.

Use your imagination to complete these sentences. Extra challenge!
Try using each of the coordinating conjunctions below at least once.

and	or	but

a. Armie visited the library every day ....

....

b. Yang considered dyeing her fur blonde ....

....

c. Plato worked on the top floor of a skyscraper ....

....

d. Oz felt queasy after riding roller coasters all day ....

....

e. Brick wanted to be a professional weightlifter ....

....

f. Shang High's ship was headed straight for an iceberg ....

....

....

g. Grit set off on a journey around

the world ....

....

....

Complex sentences have a main clause and a subordinate clause with a subordinating conjunction.

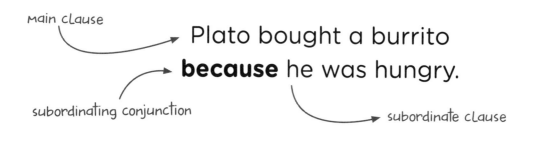

Main clause

Plato bought a burrito
because he was hungry.

subordinating conjunction

subordinate clause

REMEMBER

A **main clause** can form a complete sentence on its own but it can also form part of a compound sentence or complex sentence.

A **subordinate clause** does not make sense on its own. It adds extra information to the main clause.

Some conjunctions in complex sentences are **because, so, when, as, after** and **until**. They are used to join a main clause and a subordinate clause. They are called subordinating conjunctions.

1 **Circle the most suitable subordinating conjunction.**

a. Grit felt very unlucky   **when**   **so**   it rained on his birthday.

b. Armie gives the best advice   **until**   **because**   he is a good listener.

c. Shang High is always walking into door frames   **as**   **when**   he is so tall.

d. Brick jumped into the pool   **after**   **so**   he ate lunch.

2 Complete these complex sentences.

Use your imagination to complete these sentences.
Try to use a variety of subordinating conjunctions.

| because | so | when | as | after | until |

a. The bitter lemonade made

Plato's eyes water ....

....

....

....

....

b. Bogart spilt beans everywhere ....

....

c. Shang High lost his lucky towel ....

....

d. Yin eats oats every morning for breakfast ....

....

e. A magical genie emerged from the lamp ....

....

....

f. Brick carried a heavy briefcase everywhere ....

....

....

PUNCTUATION

When we talk, we use the tone of our voices to make our meaning clear. When we write, we rely on punctuation instead. In this chapter, you'll practise some key punctuation skills to help you make your writing more accurate and more expressive.

Commas help the reader. They can be used to separate items in a list. You need a comma between all the items except the last two. Put **and** or **or** between the last two.

Oz can sing, dance, juggle, sword-fight **and** act!

Sometimes, items in a list can be more than one word. Remember to treat these exactly the same way as a list of one-word items.

Oz can sing songs in French, dance the Macarena, juggle fourteen balls at once, sword-fight with one hand behind her back **and** act like she's a hungry lion!

1 Fix these sentences.

Add commas in the correct places.

a. Bogart wants to take over the city the country and the world.

b. Yang built a sandcastle using a bucket a spade and a lot of sand.

c. Oz hates cabbage mushrooms olives and anchovies.

d. The secret to building a robot is hard work commitment and a little bit of luck.

e. The baker whisked the eggs sieved the flour and preheated the oven to 180 degrees.

2 **Complete these sentences with lists.**
Use the words and phrases to complete the lists.
Don't forget to use commas.

a.

breakfast   lunch   and dinner

Plato loved to cook ....

....

b.

a theme park   a seaside resort   or a haunted house

For her birthday, Oz wanted to go to ....

....

c.

planted the seeds   and cut the grass   watered the plants

The gardener ....

....

3 **Now it's your turn!**
Complete this sentence by listing
five things. Use the image to help
you and don't forget to use commas.

Shang High's stomach rumbled

loudly as he looked over the

....

....

....

....

EXTRA CHALLENGE!
Use adjectives to describe the things in
your list. Instead of writing "the burger",
paint a picture for the reader and describe
it as "the juicy and succulent burger".

Remember, commas are not only used in lists. They can also be used to separate a subordinate clause from a main clause.

A **subordinate clause** does not make sense on its own. It adds extra information to the main clause and it contains a subordinating conjunction, such as **because**, **after**, **when** or **until**.

Armie happily returned to his book **after being sociable all morning.**

When a subordinate clause comes at the beginning of a sentence, it is followed by a comma.

After being sociable all morning, Armie happily returned to his book.

1 **Correct these sentences.**

Add a comma after the subordinate clause.

a. Because the fence is very tall it is difficult to see into Bogart's garden.

b. When there is lots of traffic Armie likes to listen to the radio.

2 **Rewrite these sentences so the subordinate clause comes first.**

Don't forget to add a comma.

a. Shang High lived in a very small cottage until he won the lottery.

....

b. Plato would keep baking cakes until he found the perfect recipe.

....

Commas are also used after fronted adverbials.

Adverbial phrases describe how, when or where a verb happens. When these adverbial phrases go at the start of a sentence and add extra information, they are called **fronted adverbials**.

Fronted adverbials are always followed by a comma that separates them from the rest of the sentence, for example:

All of a sudden, the thief vanished in a puff of smoke.

1 **Correct these sentences by adding commas after the fronted adverbials.**

a. In his secret lair Bogart devised a cunning plan.

b. After hours of work Grit finally perfected the wheel.

c. By midnight Oz's phone had run out of battery.

2 **Now it's your turn!**
Write a sentence with a fronted adverbial to describe the image below. Don't forget to use a comma.

....

....

....

....

....

Writing with speech can be confusing because
we often have a sentence within a sentence.

Sometimes, it's helpful to think about the sentence
as split into the **speech sentence** and the **real sentence**.

speech
sentence   "I love music!" announced Shang High.   real
sentence

DID YOU KNOW?

Inverted commas are also
known as speech marks.

Inverted commas go at the **start** and **end**
of speech. There is always a punctuation
mark before the final inverted comma.

If the speech
sentence is a question,
use a **question mark**.

"Who are   Yin asked,
you?"   "Who are
asked Yin.   you?"

If the speech sentence is
an exclamation sentence, has
a strong feeling or is said loudly,
use an **exclamation mark**.

"Stop it!"   Grit shouted,
shouted Grit.   "Stop it!"

If the speech sentence
is a statement and comes at
the **start of the real sentence**,
use a **comma**.

"We're sorry,"
said Bogart.

If the speech sentence
is a statement and comes at
the **end of the real sentence**,
use a **full stop**.

Bogart said,
"We're sorry."

When the **speech sentence comes at the end of the real sentence**, you need
to add a **comma** before it. This is the case for all speech sentence types.

1 **Fix these sentences by adding punctuation.**

Add inverted commas and add a suitable punctuation mark before each final inverted comma. Remember to add a comma before the speech if it comes second.

a. I'm sorry whispered Yin.

b. Where is the library asked Armie.

c. Stop it yelled Oz.

d. Plato said This soup is too salty.

2 **Rewrite the speech in the bubbles as full sentences.**

Don't forget to use inverted commas and a punctuation mark before the final inverted comma. Write at least one sentence with the speech second and remember to add a comma before the speech.

a. "I'm bored," grumbled Grit.

Grit

I'm bored.

Shang High

Why are all ceilings so low?

EXTRA CHALLENGE!

Try using a different word for "said" each time.

b.

c.

Let's take over the world!

Bogart

Apostrophes can be used to show contraction or possession.

Sometimes, apostrophes can show where letters are missing in shortened versions of words.

These shortened versions of words are called contractions.

REMEMBER!

Sometimes, the contraction does not exactly match the words that it is made from.
For example, will not = won't.

You will love
contractions.

You'll love
contractions.

1 Draw lines to match the words to their contractions.

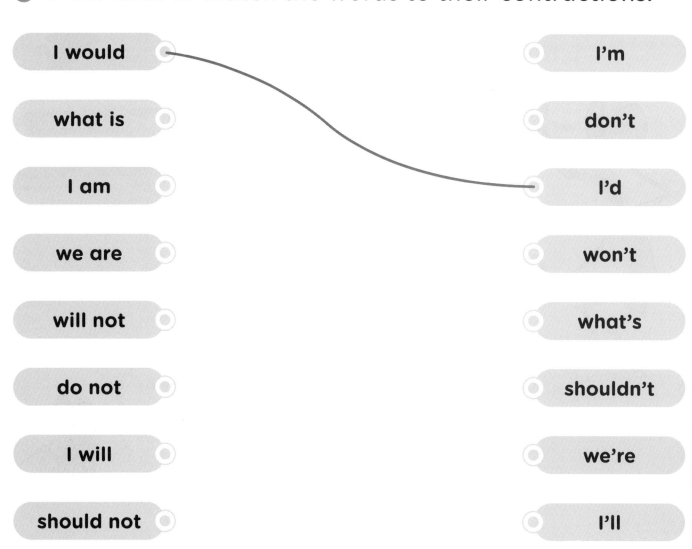

I would	I'm
what is	don't
I am	I'd
we are	won't
will not	what's
do not	shouldn't
I will	we're
should not	I'll

2 **Rewrite these sentences with the correct contraction.**

a. **I would** love some whipped cream please!

....

b. "**Do not** move!" shouted the detective.

....

c. **I am** very happy to see you!

....

d. "**We are** in this together!" Bearnice told Oz.

....

e. **What is** your favourite ice cream flavour?

....

f. Yang **should not** have lied to Yin!

....

g. "I **will not** do this again," promised Bogart.

....

h. **She is** the first ostrich to win this award!

....

3 Can you help fix the mistakes in bold?

Bearnice is muddled! She wrote an **email to the President of the National Cheese Convention**, but she wrote it in informal language when she should have written it in formal language.

Formal language is used when writing to people you don't know well, or people you want to show respect to. You do not usually use contractions in formal writing.

Edit the writing so that this formal letter has no contractions.

Dear President of the National Cheese Convention,

I am

~~I'm~~ writing to you to express my concern about the state of cheese today. I **don't** want to alarm you, but I was in my local supermarket the other day and I noticed several cheeses that were more hole than cheese! I **didn't** expect to see the day when the holes in cheese outgrew the cheese itself. This **shouldn't** have happened. **I'd** like to meet with you to discuss this state of affairs as soon as possible.

Yours faithfully,

Bearnice

4 Can you help fix the mistakes in bold?

Bearnice is muddled, AGAIN! She wrote a **text to her friend**, but she wrote it in formal language when she should have written it in informal language.

Informal language is used in more casual situations. It is often more friendly and more personal. Here, you can use contractions.

Edit the writing so the informal text has contractions.

Hey Shang High,

You **will not** believe what has happened. I know **we are** meant to

be going ice skating today, but **I am** too upset about the state of

the cheese in the supermarket. I think **I will** stay at home.

See you soon,

Bearnice

Apostrophes can be used to show contraction or possession.

You can show that something belongs to someone (or something) by using an **apostrophe** and an **-s**.

There are four rules about how you can do this.

You may remember that for most **singular nouns**, we add an **apostrophe** and an **-s**.

Shang High's neck is very long.

It's trickier when **singular nouns end in -s**. In these cases, we add an **apostrophe only**.

Please water **James'** plants.
The **class'** homework is late.

When a noun has a **regular plural** (ending in **-s**), to show belonging you add an **apostrophe only**.

The **cats'** tails are very soft.

However, some **irregular plural nouns** (like one woman, many women) do not end in **-s**. Here, you add an **apostrophe** and an **-s**.

The **women's** library is open.

1 **Rewrite these sentences as phrases.**

Use an apostrophe to show belonging.

a. The pile of books belongs to Armie.

Armie's pile of books.

b. The office belongs to the business.

c. The suitcase belongs to Bearnice.

d. The salon belongs to the hairdressers.

e. The cheese belongs to the mice.

f. The television belongs to the family.

2 **Now it's your turn!**

Write a sentence containing a possessive apostrophe to describe the image.

It's and its look similar, but mean very different things.

It's is a contraction meaning **it is** or **it has.**

It's three o'clock.
It's not stopped snowing!

Its means **belonging to it.**

The tree has a kite stuck to its branch.

1 Circle the correct spelling of it's or its.

If you aren't sure, try reading the sentence out loud using **it is** or **it has** to see if it makes sense.

a. **Its**   **It's**   almost time for bed.

b. The ghost had slime all over   **its**   **it's**   face.

c. This afternoon,   **its**   **it's**   going to rain heavily.

d. The train had   **its**   **it's**   wheels painted for the

third time this week.

2 Rewrite these sentences.

Expand the contraction **it's** to **it is** or **it has**, using the rest of the sentence (the context) to work out which makes the most sense.

a. It's never snowed in the summer before!

....

b. "It's my birthday tomorrow," sang Oz.

....

You're and your look similar and sound the same, but mean very different things.

You're is a contraction of **you are**.

You're riding my bike.

Your means **belonging to you**.

I am riding your bike.

1 ## Complete these sentences with you're or your.

Read it aloud with the expanded form of the contraction to see which makes sense.

a. Where are you going on (**your**) (**you're**) holiday?

b. (**Your**) (**You're**) never going to win!" mocked Yang.

c. When did you last visit (**your**) (**you're**) dentist?

d. (**Your**) (**You're**) hilarious!

e. "Can I borrow (**your**) (**you're**) shoes?" asked Bearnice.

f. "... but I'm (**your**) (**you're**) sister!" whined Yin.

g. (**Your**) (**You're**) always late!

h. Put down (**your**) (**you're**) pens. The exam is over.

Ellipsis (plural ellipses) is a punctuation mark consisting of **three dots** (...).

There is not always a right or wrong way to use an ellipsis. Authors make choices about how to use them to make something more exciting for the reader. When you are writing, you have to make decisions like that too!

1

To **create suspense** by adding a pause at the end of a sentence.

Then, all the lights went out...

2

To show the **trailing off** of a thought.

"I'm not sure what to..." Bearnice began.

3

To show where a **word or words have been removed** from a text quote to shorten it.

Main quote

Brick loved to exercise all of his muscles but sometimes he needed a day off.

→

shortened quote

Brick loved to exercise... but sometimes he needed a day off.

1 Fill in the gaps.

Use either an ellipsis or a full stop.

a. "I can't remember .... " replied Shang High ....

b. All of a sudden, the aliens arrived ....

2 Fill in the gaps in this shortened quote.

Use either an ellipsis or a full stop.

Main quote: Watermelons grow best in warm conditions and are believed to have originated in Africa.

Shortened quote:

Watermelons .... are believed to have originated in Africa ....

3 **Read each sentence and identify what the ellipsis is being used for.**

Draw lines to match the sentence to the type of ellipsis use.

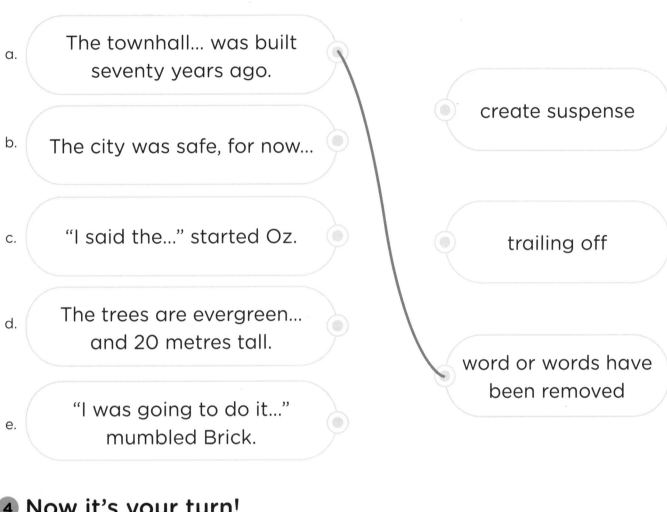

a. The townhall... was built seventy years ago.

b. The city was safe, for now...

c. "I said the..." started Oz.

d. The trees are evergreen... and 20 metres tall.

e. "I was going to do it..." mumbled Brick.

create suspense

trailing off

word or words have been removed

4 **Now it's your turn!**

Can you write two sentences that use ellipses to create suspense and make your reader desperate to know what happens next (sometimes called a **cliffhanger**)? Your sentences could be about anything that makes you feel scared or tense, like walking in the woods at night or opening a secret door.

a. ....

....

....

b. ....

....

....

Paragraphs make your writing easier to read by grouping together ideas in sections.

New paragraphs always start on a new line. In narrative writing, they can be used to group ideas according to **time**, **person** or **place**.

Let's have a look at two paragraphs from the same fiction text. Using your knowledge about paragraphs, describe out loud why the paragraphs change when they do:

After months of training, Bearnice finally felt ready to climb the world's tallest mountain. It took her four days to reach the top, but the elation she felt as she stepped onto the peak made it all worth it. She had done it.

An hour later, Bearnice began to realise her mistake. She had spent months training to climb up the mountain, but she had no idea how to climb back down. This was going to be a very difficult descent.

1 Add the paragraph breaks.

In fiction (or narrative writing), it can be difficult to remember when to start a new paragraph. You might start a new paragraph when you have a jump in time or place.

When we edit, we add // to show when a new paragraph should begin. Here is the beginning of a fiction story in which four paragraphs have been squashed together. Read the text and decide where the new paragraphs should begin. The first one has been done for you, so there are two more paragraph breaks for you to add in.

Plato had worked at the doughnut factory for as long as he could remember. He loved making doughnuts. He loved weighing out the ingredients, mixing them together, frying the dough and, most importantly of all, decorating them. The factory had three signature flavours: Original Glazed, Strawberry Jam and Triple Chocolate Delight. // One day, the owner of the factory, Brick, made an announcement that changed everything. "As of today, we will no longer be making Triple Chocolate Delight. Instead, we will be making my new favourite flavour, Salmon Surprise!" declared Brick. Outside of the factory, no one wanted to hang out with Plato anymore because he constantly stank of salmon. The smell was sickening, the taste was even worse and the smooth icing was now filled with slimy scales. One week later, Plato decided enough was enough. He needed to take a stand. When he arrived at the factory, he began to cry, "No more salmon! No more salmon!" The entire factory joined in with the chanting. If they all worked together, Plato felt as though they had the power to get rid of Salmon Surprise for good.

In non-fiction writing, paragraphs are often organised by topic.
A topic can be anything from carrots to manicures to modern art.

Let's have a look at two paragraphs from the same non-fiction text.
Using your knowledge about paragraphs, describe out loud why the
paragraphs change when they do:

The smallest dinosaur is the Lesothosaurus.
This bird-like herbivore was the size of a chicken.
It got its name from Lesotho, a country in Africa,
where early fossils were uncovered.

The largest dinosaur is the Argentinosaurus.
It weighed 77 tonnes, the equivalent of 17 elephants.
It is the largest land animal to have ever lived.

1 Which sentences could be in the same paragraph?

These sentences are all taken from a text about penguins. Draw lines
to match sentences that could be in the same paragraph. Remember
to read through all the options first.

Penguin feet are adapted
to walk long distances.

The greatest concentrations
are on the Antarctic coasts.

Penguins are only found in
the Southern Hemisphere.

These feathers are
short and dense.

Penguins eat silverfish,
krill and squid.

They have four toes, unlike
the five typical of mammals.

Penguins have black
and white feathers.

Adult penguins eat 2–3
kilograms of fish per day.

2 # Now it's your turn!

Plan three paragraphs on the topic of '**My daily routine**'.
Use the subheadings to guide you, and plan what you want
to write about using a list of three bullet points per section.

My morning routine

· Brush my teeth

My school routine

My evening routine

Headings and subheadings are titles that tell the reader about the text. They are usually found in non-fiction. A **heading** tells the reader about the **main topic** of the text.

If the text is split up into smaller sections, these may have **subheadings** to tell the reader what the **smaller section** is about.

Headings and subheadings can be single words, phrases or full sentences. These different types of titles make the text clearer and easier to read.

1 Match the paragraph to the subheading.

The heading of these paragraphs is **Fruit**.
Draw lines to label each paragraph with a suitable subheading.

FRUIT

 Apples

 Pineapples

 Bananas

a.

These long, yellow fruits are grown in hot, tropical climates including America, India, China and Africa. This fruit is soft and sweet, making it perfect for baking with. It is also a good source of potassium.

b.

Used in crumbles and pies, this sweet and crunchy fruit grows best in climates with cold winters and moderate summers. They commonly grow in the colours red or green, depending on the variety.

c.

Indigenous to South America, this fruit is known as "ananas" in many languages. Recognisable for its spiky green leaves and rough yellow skin, the fruit is sweet, tart and juicy.

2 **What subheadings would you give each of these paragraphs?**
These paragraphs are from a longer text called **The World's Strangest Conventions**. Choose a suitable subheading for each one.

DID YOU KNOW?
A convention is a conference or gathering of people to discuss or engage in a common interest.

a.

Starting in Ohio in 1976, the Twins Days Festival is held every year in August. Almost 3,000 people attend every year, most of whom are twins. The attendees usually come with other members of their family, with ages ranging from newborns to 90-year-olds.

b.

Held in Nevada since 1991, the International UFO Congress Convention discusses alien abductions, UFO sightings, crop circles, conspiracies and more. The event usually has over thirty speakers and lasts for a full week.

c.

Created by the World Toilet Organisation, the World Toilet Summit was first launched in Singapore in 2001. The purpose of the convention is to bring sanitation and clean water to the billions of people around the world who still need it. The convention has travelled to various cities around the world including Beijing, Belfast and Moscow.

VOCABULARY

The older you get and the more vocabulary you learn, the more you develop your word consciousness. Word consciousness refers to your awareness of the connections between words (like synonyms, antonyms and shades of meaning) as well as how words are built from various parts (like Greek and Latin roots, prefixes and suffixes). The deeper your word consciousness, the better you are at interpreting unfamiliar words when you come across them, which gives you the ability to read an endless supply of life-changing books whenever you want.

Prefixes are letters or groups of letters that are added to the beginning of words to change their meaning.

The prefix **in-** usually means **not**.
in ✛ accurate ═ **inaccurate**, meaning **not accurate**

The prefix **in-** sometimes changes to **il-**, **im-** or **ir-**.

Use **il-** when the root word begins with an **l-**.
il ✛ literate ═ **illiterate**
meaning **not literate**
(not able to read)

Use **im-** when the root words begins with **b-**, **m-** or **p-**.
im ✛ possible ═ **impossible**
meaning **not possible**

Use **ir-** when the root word begins with **r-**.
ir ✛ relevant ═ **irrelevant**
meaning **not relevant**

1 Transform these stories with the right prefix!

Pick the correct root word from the options below and add the prefix **ir-**, **il-**, **in-** or **im-**. Then, write the complete word in the gap and say it aloud to check if it sounds right. The first one has been done for you.

| correct | responsible | ~~legal~~ | visible | perfect |

a. Despite how incredible Shang High's art was, graffiti was still

illegal .

b. "I think I've been given the

.... order!"

cried Bearnice as she watched

Bogart swim in her cereal.

c. Armie had an excellent holiday,

despite the ....

weather.

d. It was .... of

Armie to fly his aeroplane during

the storm.

e. Sometimes, Yin wishes she was

....

The prefix **re-** means **again** or **back**.

re + play = **replay**
meaning **play again**

re + pay = **repay**
meaning **pay back**

The prefix **anti-** means **not** or **against**.

anti + viral = **antiviral**
meaning **against viruses**

anti + social = **antisocial**
meaning **not social**

① Transform these stories with the right prefix!

Pick the correct prefix and write the whole word in the gap to complete the sentence. Say it out loud to make sure it makes sense.

a. Armie was feeling

.... so he

hid in the corner.

re-   anti- social

b. When Plato finally got to open

the enormous present, it was

a real ....

re-   anti- climax

REMEMBER!

Prefixes are letters or groups of letters that are added to the beginning of words to change their meaning.

c. Oz was going to have to

.... her

surfing plans.

re- **anti-** think

d. The ....

suits allowed them to

experience true weightlessness.

re- **anti-** gravity

e. Grit was ....

himself with a classy new look.

re- **anti-** inventing

The prefix **inter-** usually means **among** or **between**.

inter + national = **international**

meaning existing **between nations**

The prefix **auto-** usually means **self** or **own**.

auto + biography = **autobiography**

meaning a **self-written biography** (a book about the person's life story)

1 Transform these stories with the right prefix!

Pick the correct prefix and write the whole word in the gap to complete the sentence. Say it out loud to make sure it makes sense.

a. Plato really did not want to

.... with

Bogart today.

auto-　**inter-** act

b. After winning, Armie knew he

would have to sign a lot of

....

auto-　**inter-** graphs

REMEMBER!

Prefixes are Letters or groups of Letters that are added to the beginning of words to change their meaning.

c. Aliens are the best companions for

.... travel.

auto-   inter-   stellar

d. Armie was only able to complete the mission because his spaceship was on

....

auto-   inter-   pilot

e. The best part about

.... travel was the bustling, local markets.

auto-   inter-   city

Some words are made up of different parts, such as **prefixes** (letters added to the beginning of a word), **suffixes** (letters added to the end of a word) and **roots**. The root is the main part of the word and carries the meaning. Many root words, prefixes and suffixes in the English language originate from Greek and Latin. Understanding what these mean can help you work out the meaning of a word in English.

For example, the Greek root word **phone** means **sound**.

tele**phone**
n. a device used to send **sound** over long distances by wire or radio waves

homo**phone**s
n. words that **sound** the same but are spelled differently and have different meanings

From now on, if you ever see a word with **phone**, you will know that it is probably related to the Greek root word and means something to do with **sound**.

TIP!

When we notice things like root words, prefixes and suffixes, it helps develop our word consciousness. This is our awareness of words that helps us to spell and learn new vocabulary.

1 **Recognising different parts of a word is the perfect skill for a vocabulary detective.**
Let's get practising!

a. The Greek root **biblio** means book.
The suffix **phile** means a person who likes or loves.
What do you think **bibliophile** means?

b. The Greek root **arachne** means spider.
The Greek root **phobia** means fear.
What do you think **arachnophobia** means?

....

c. The Latin prefix **bi** means two.
The Latin root **lingua** means language.
What do you think **bilingual** means?

....

d. The Greek root **astron** means star.
The Greek suffix **logy** means the study of something.
What do you think **astrology** means?

....

2 **Let's practise more!**
Read the 'evidence' and draw your conclusion
about what each root word means.

a. An auto**bio**graphy is a self-written book about a person's life.
Biology is the study of life and living things.
What do you think **bio** means?

....

b. A **mono**cle is a single eyeglass.
A **mono**logue is a speech delivered by one person.
What do you think **mono** means?

....

c. A **nov**ice is someone new to a job or situation.
A **nov**elty is something new.
What do you think **nov** means?

....

Synonyms are words that mean the same or nearly the same as another word. When you want to be more precise and show shades of meaning, choosing the right synonym is an excellent way to do it!

① Each word has two synonyms. Can you join them up?

Draw a line to connect the synonyms. The first one is done for you.

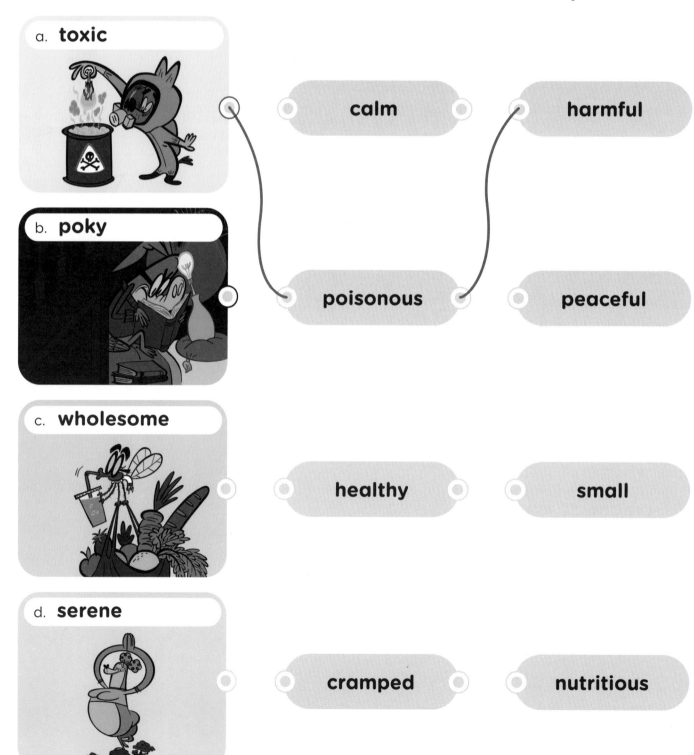

a. **toxic**

b. **poky**

c. **wholesome**

d. **serene**

calm

harmful

poisonous

peaceful

healthy

small

cramped

nutritious

② Find the synonyms in these sentences.

Underline the two words in each one that have a similar meaning.

a. The uneven track resulted in a very bumpy journey into town.

b. Brick only ate a tiny slice of pie. He was still hungry because it was so minuscule.

c. Bearnice was worried about the dangerous effects of harmful pollutants.

③ Can you improve this story?

The descriptive vocabulary in this story could be more exciting. Cross out the words you want to replace and write a more interesting synonym above them. Try to replace at least three of the adjectives in the text. Use the words below to help you. The first one is done for you.

| gigantic | delicious | difficult | starving | glistening |
| enormous | tough | burning | exhausted | parched |

difficult

The journey up the river was <u>hard</u>. Big waves rocked the boat

and the sun's rays were hot. Yin felt tired. Yang felt hungry.

Yang looked into the water and saw some fish with

shiny scales swimming below. She licked

her dry lips and thought about the

yummy dinner she would eat later on.

An antonym is a word that means the opposite of another word.

For example, **good** and **bad** are antonyms.

1 Circle the antonyms.

a. Circle the antonym of bland.

tasty   bumpy   boring

b. Circle the antonym of gleeful.

happy   luxurious   miserable

c. Circle the antonym of loathe.

hate   enjoy   distract

d. Circle the antonym of backbreaking.

tough   ridiculous   easy

2 Draw a line to connect the antonyms.

blunt	far
fear	modern
alone	guilty
beginning	burning
artificial	sharp
arrival	natural
maximum	sweet
innocent	together
near	end
ancient	departure
freezing	courage
bitter	minimum

Homophones are words that **sound the same** but are **spelled differently** and have **different meanings**. Near homophones are words that **sound similar** but are spelled differently and have different meanings.

This page introduces lots of different homophones and near homophones. Read through them and try to remember as many as you can because they will help you complete the next few activities. If you need some help later on, you can look back to this page for a reminder!

flour *(n.)*

flower *(n.)*

herd (n.) – A **herd** of elephants wandered into town.

heard (v.) – I **heard** some excellent news.

grown (v.) – My sunflower has **grown** taller than me!

groan (v.) – She let out a **groan** and turned off the TV.

write *(v.)*

right *(adj.)*

peace *(n.)*

piece *(n.)*

wandered (v.) – I **wandered** over the hills for days.

wondered (v.) – He **wondered** whether he'd ever see her again.

jeans (n.)

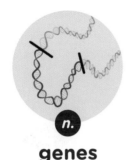

genes (n.)

aloud (*adv.*) – I prefer reading **aloud** to reading in my head.

allowed (*adj.*) – How many slices of cake are we **allowed** to take?

effect (*n.*) – The hypnosis had no **effect** on him.

affect (*v.*) – The hurricane will **affect** many countries.

band (n.)

banned (adj.)

mousse (n.)

moose (n.)

weather (*n.*) – Always carry an umbrella because the **weather** is unpredictable.

whether (*conj.*) – I'm going to the party **whether** you like it or not!

accept (*v.*) – Please **accept** my apology.

except (*prep.*) – Everyone is invited **except** me.

knight (n.)

night (n.)

1 **Circle the homophone that matches the picture.**

TIP!

Trying to remember these spellings now will help you remember them in the long term. However, if you get stuck, you can look back to the first page.

a.

aloud

allowed

b.

mousse

moose

c.

weather

whether

d.

peace

piece

e.

genes

jeans

f.

knight

night

g.

herd

heard

h.

flour

flower

2 **Complete the sentences with the correct word.**

Choose the correct spelling and fill in the blanks.

a. Oz rang the bubble gum factory and gave them

a .... of her mind.

  piece   peace

b. Plato came from a long line of chefs. Cooking was in his

....

  jeans   genes

c. Microplastics may be small, but they have a devastating

.... on the planet.

  affect   effect

d. It wasn't long before they .... stink bombs.

  band   banned

e. There was nothing to do .... sit back and

relax.

  except   accept

f. The tastiest bananas are .... in tropical

countries.

  grown   groan

3 Match the homophones to the pictures!

The words below are homophones. This means that they sound the same but are spelled differently and have different meanings. Draw a line connecting each word to the right picture.

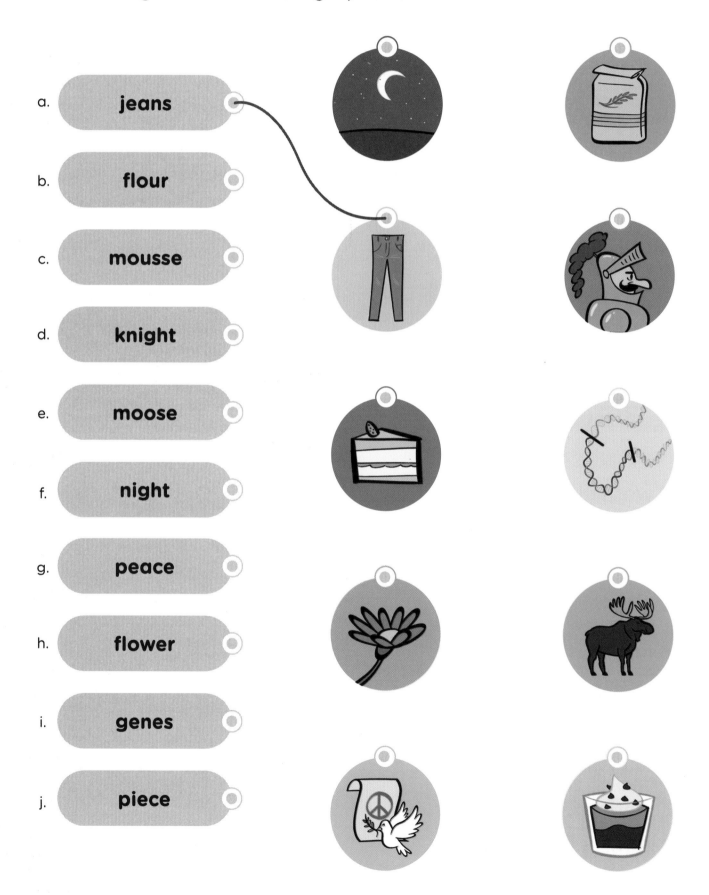

a. jeans

b. flour

c. mousse

d. knight

e. moose

f. night

g. peace

h. flower

i. genes

j. piece

4 Complete these sentences.

Fill in the gaps with the word **effect** or **affect**.

TIP!

Effect is a noun and affect is a verb. This can be tricky, so think about what the word is doing in the sentence. Is it a verb or is it a noun?

a. Spilling lemonade all over

my experiment will definitely

.... the results.

b. Listening to loud music can have a negative

.... on your hearing.

c. The dreadful weather will .... my

weekend plans.

d. The medicine had an ....

on the patient's symptoms.

e. The rising price of chocolate bars will ....

the number of children visiting the shop.

f. Pollution has a harmful .... on the

environment.

Multiple-meaning words are words that have the same spelling and usually sound alike, but have different meanings.

Bearnice **left** through the door on the **left**.

Here, Left means to exit or Leave

Here, Left means the opposite of right

DID YOU KNOW?

Multiple-meaning words are also called homonyms.

① Spot the multiple-meaning words.

Read these sentences and underline the multiple-meaning words. Describe out loud the two different meanings.

a. Without his glasses on, Armie did not realise he had put the bowls on the shelf that was meant for glasses.

b. "Duck!" yelled Brick, as a duck came hurtling towards the canoe.

c. Bearnice wanted to do the right thing. She thought Oz had a right to know that her jumper was inside out.

d. In the spring, as the flowers blossom and the days get longer, you might notice an extra spring in Grit's step.

2 Match the sentences to the correct images.

These sentences each contain a homonym. Draw lines to match each sentence to the correct image.

a. Brick bought a new watch.

REMEMBER!

Homonyms look and sound the same, so use the context clues in the sentences to work out their meanings.

b. Plato wanted to watch TV.

c. Armie paddled away from the enormous wave.

d. A wave can mean hello or goodbye.

e. Bearnice soaked the casserole dish in the kitchen sink.

f. Nobody thought the ship would sink.

A synonym is a word that means the same
or nearly the same as another word.

Some words have similar meanings,
but one is stronger than the other.

Yin was **pleased** when
she finished the race
in second place.

Yang was **euphoric**
when she finished
the race first.

The words **pleased** and **euphoric** both have a similar meaning
to the word **happy**, but you might use **euphoric** when you
are talking about feeling **really, really happy**.

Meticulous is more
careful than **thorough**.

Minuscule is
smaller than **tiny**.

Preposterous is
sillier than **absurd**.

1 Which sentence uses the strongest synonym?

Read the sentences and answer the questions. These synonyms may mean the same or nearly the same as another word, but one is stronger than the other.

a. **On Tuesday, the sun was hot.**
On Wednesday, it was scorching.
Which day was hotter?

....

b. **Yin was disappointed.**
Yang was heartbroken.
Who felt worse?

....

c. **The German cheese had a strong smell.**
The Italian cheese had an overpowering smell.
Which was the smellier cheese?

....

d. **The thunderstorm was devastating.**
The sandstorm was inconvenient.
Which storm was more of a nuisance?

....

e. **Oz was speechless.**
Brick was surprised.
Who was more shocked?

....

f. **Bogart found the performance awkward.**
Bearnice thought it was excruciating.
Who had a worse time at the theatre?

....

Vocabulary has the power to transform any piece of writing into something exciting. Take this simple sentence:

The girl ran towards the roller coaster.

By adding some adjectives and replacing a few of the words, the sentence is completely transformed. Now, it tells the reader a lot more about what happened:

The girl **sprinted as fast as she could** towards the **colossal** roller coaster.

You need all kinds of words to tell stories. In this section, we'll learn some words to help you describe **nature**. We'll also learn some words that you can use instead of **surprised** and instead of **said**, because repeating the same words all the time can get boring.

Knowing these words will also help you with your reading, because they are words you are likely to come across in books.

Next to each word you will find a list of **synonyms** and **word pairs** and an empty table with two columns. Sort each word in the list into the correct column.

A **synonym** is a word that means the same or nearly the same as another word.

Word pairs (or collocates) are words that are often found together in speech or in writing, like **light backpack** or **light snow**.

light backpack

light snow

1

ideal	setting	perfect
countryside	blissful	childhood

synonyms	word pairs
perfect	childhood

idyllic

adj. ideal or perfect;
like a beautiful place where
everything is just as it should be

Extra challenge! Can you write a sentence using the word **idyllic**?

2

healthy	luxurious	garden
rich	greenery	rainforest

synonyms	word pairs

lush

adj. rich, overgrown or
luxurious; like a garden full
of big, healthy plants

Extra challenge! Can you write a sentence using the word **lush**?

1

silence   expression   spectator
shocked   amazed   surprised

synonyms	word pairs

astonished

adj. surprised or amazed; like when you've seen something you can't believe

Can you write a sentence using the word **astonished**?

2

shocked   astonished   surprised
reaction   audience   onlooker

synonyms	word pairs

flabbergasted

adj. shocked or amazed; like how you would feel if you won the lottery

Can you write a sentence using the word **flabbergasted**?

3

stare	disbelieving	silence
reaction	unconvinced	doubtful

synonyms	word pairs

incredulous

adj. disbelieving or doubtful;
when you can't believe
your eyes

Can you write a sentence using the word **incredulous**?

4

dazed	stupefied	amazed
surprise	expression	silence

synonyms	word pairs

stunned

adj. amazed or stupefied;
like being so surprised you
instantly freeze

Can you write a sentence using the word **stunned**?

1

blabbed　accidentally　exclaimed

suddenly　awkwardly　let slip

synonyms	word pairs

blurted

v. cried out or said suddenly;
like shouting out when it's
someone else's turn

Can you write a sentence using the word **blurted**?

2

buzzed　monotonously　away

murmured　endlessly　hummed

synonyms	word pairs

droned

v. hummed or talked endlessly
in a dull voice; like reading out
a boring list

Can you write a sentence using the word **droned**?

3

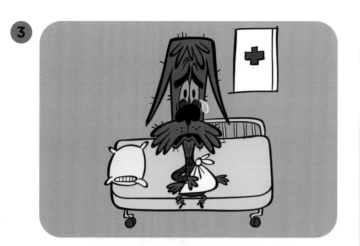

whimpered

v. whined or sniffled; like making a soft, crying sound when you're sad or in pain

| whined | feebly | sniffled |
| sadly | moaned | softly |

synonyms	word pairs

Can you write a sentence using the word **whimpered**?

4

squealed

v. wailed or yelped; like the high-pitched sound you make when you're taken by surprise

| shrieked | loudly | wailed |
| shrilly | excitedly | yelped |

synonyms	word pairs

Can you write a sentence using the word **squealed**?

In the English language, there are many well-known **idioms**.
These are phrases or expressions that are used for their
figurative meaning, rather than their **literal** meaning.

A **literal meaning** is when a phrase stays true to its actual meaning.
A **figurative meaning** is when a phrase means something more than
the most obvious interpretation.

The literal meaning of **a piece of cake** is:

But the idiom **a piece of cake** also has the figurative meaning
of **easy to do**. For example, **This exam is a piece of cake!**

You may have heard of many of these idioms.
They can be used to add style and character to writing
or to express complex ideas in a simple way.

on cloud nine	→	very happy
break a leg	→	good luck (often said to someone about to perform)
elephant in the room	→	a large, obvious problem that is avoided in discussion
once in a blue moon	→	very rarely
two peas in a pod	→	very similar, particularly in appearance
spill the beans	→	reveal secret information

1 **Rewrite these sentences replacing the words in bold with an idiom.**
Use the idioms on the opposite page or any others you already know!

a. Brick and Armie avoided discussing Bogart's plans to take over the world. It was the **huge issue that they were avoiding**.

....

....

....

b. Sometimes, Bearnice struggles to tell Yin and Yang apart. They really are **very similar**.

....

....

c. Plato was desperate to know Grit's secret, and Oz was ready to **reveal the secret**.

....

....

d. Brick felt **incredibly happy** as he finished the marathon an hour before anyone else.

....

....

e. Oz was terrible at juggling but Shang High thought it was **very easy**.

....

....

A **proverb** (also called an adage) is a short saying that
is generally accepted to have some truth to it.

These short sayings are philosophical and their ideas are universal.

An example of a proverb would be, **actions speak louder than words**,
meaning that what a person does is more important than what
they say they will do.

1 Match the proverb to its definition.

Use the clues in the definitions to work out
the meaning of these proverbs.

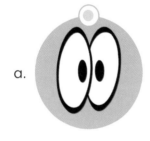

a.

**Beauty is in the eye
of the beholder.**

If you start
something early,
you will have
an advantage
over others.

b.

**The early bird
catches the
worm.**

c.

**Practice
makes
perfect.**

Regularly doing
something is
the best way for
you to improve.

Everyone has their
own view on what
is beautiful.

d. **Don't judge a book by its cover.**

c. **Two wrongs don't make a right.**

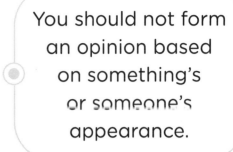

You should not form an opinion based on something's or someone's appearance.

You should not criticise a gift, even if you do not like it.

f. **Don't count your chickens before they're hatched.**

You should never hurt someone, even if they have hurt you.

You should not count on something until it is certain.

g. **Two heads are better than one.**

h. **Never look a gift horse in the mouth.**

You will make better decisions if you ask for advice.

SPELLING

Using the correct spelling of a word helps your reader understand exactly what you mean. In this chapter, you'll master some challenging spelling rules, some less common spellings of familiar sounds and some common exception words that don't follow the rules.

The hard /k/ sound is often written as **c**, **k** or **ck**.
This sound can also be written as **ch**,
like in **chemist** or **stomach**.

The hard /k/ written as **ch** can be found at the beginning
or the end of a word. Unfortunately, there is no rule that tells
you when to use this spelling. It's just one of those things you
have to know. So, let's get some practice!

1 **Circle the words that have a /k/ sound written as ch.**

technology

moustache

choose

character

chemical

challenging

2 **Complete the table.**

Underline the letters that make the /k/ sound in each word in the box.
Then, write the words under the matching spelling pattern.

ache	cart	unmistakable	sock
anchor	echo	snowflake	prank

c	ck	k	ch

3 **Circle the correct spelling of the words in bold.**

a. "Drop the **anchor**   **ancor** at once!" yelled Bearnice.

"I must swim!"

b. Bogart was planning a monumental **prank**   **pranch** .

c. Brick stuck out his tongue to catch a **snowflake**   **snowflache** .

d. The **unmistachable**   **unmistakable** sound of Brick's

footsteps shook the house.

e. The supersized milkshake had given Shang High

a severe tummy **ache**   **ake** .

f. Plato's voice **echoed**

ekoed through the

hollow tree trunk.

We've seen how **ch** can make a hard /k/ sound.
The letters **ch** can also make a /sh/ sound
(most often written as **sh**, **ss** or **s**).

In English, words that use the **ch** spelling
of the /sh/ sound usually come from French.

1 Circle the words that have
a /sh/ sound written as **ch**.

| chorus | chandelier | machine |

| chimpanzee | moustache | arch |

2 Complete the table.

Underline the letters that make the /sh/ sound in each word in the box.
Then, write the words under the matching spelling pattern.

sugar	issue	parachute
wash	nonchalant	tissue
chef	brochure	sure

sh	ss	s	ch

3 **Circle the correct spelling of the words in bold.**

a. It didn't say anything about giant rats in the **broshure**

brochure .

b. Bearnice noticed the hole in her **parachute** **parassute**

far too late.

c. Plato was an experimental **shef** **chef** .

d. Yin had a real **issue** **ichue** with being called

a cat instead of a tiger.

e. When Oz looked up from the pick'n'mix, her entire

face was covered in **chugar** **sugar** .

f. Shang High looked

extremely **nonchalant**

nonshalant about the

whole crocodile situation.

The hard /g/ sound is usually written with a **g** or a **gg**, but can sometimes be written as -**gue** at the end of words, like in **league** or **vague**.

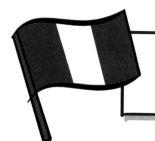

DID YOU KNOW?

Words that include the "gue" spelling of the hard /g/ sound usually came into the English Language from French.

1 Complete the table.

Underline the letters that make the hard /g/ sound in each word in the box. Then, write the words under the matching spelling pattern.

catalogue	jogged	league	begin
bigger	shrug	plugged	dialogue
brag	intrigued	plague	monologue

g	gg	gue

2 **Can you unscramble the words in bold?**

a. There were 40 outbreaks of the **pgalue** ....

between 1348 and 1665.

b. Grit's team won and went straight to the top of the **leugea**

....

c. Yin ordered five pairs of new trainers from the **cataleguo**

....

3 **Circle the correct spelling of the words in bold.**

a. The (**dialoge**) (**dialogue**) between the two main

characters was very funny!

b. Shang High (**plugued**) (**plugged**) in the speaker

and pressed play.

c. Oz was (**intrigued**) (**intriged**) by the anonymous poem.

d. All Bearnice could do was (**shrug**) (**shrugue**) because

she didn't know the answer.

TIP!

In words where –gue comes after an n, like tongue or meringue, the sound made is the same as the sound in song or bling.

The hard /k/ sound is usually written as **c**, **k**, or **ck**, but can sometimes be written as **-que** at the end of words, like in **mosque** or **plaque**.

DID YOU KNOW?

Words that include the "que" spelling of the /k/ sound usually came into the English Language from French.

1 Underline the /k/ sound.

Underline the letters that make the /k/ sound in each word.
The first one is done for you. Then write out each word three times.

a. uni<u>que</u> ....

b. sleek ....

c. mystique ....

d. attack ....

2 Complete the table.

Underline the letters that make the /k/ sound in each word in the box.
Then, write the words under the matching spelling pattern.

> spark   grotesque   unique   opaque   feedback
>
> oak   antique   flock   careful

c	ck	k	que

3 Circle the correct spelling of the words in bold.

a. Say what you like but Bearnice's singing voice was certainly

unike   unique   unick   .

b. Oz loved her new   sleek   sleeque   sleeck   bicycle.

c. The car windows were entirely   opaque   opake   opack   .

d. Armie handled the priceless   anticke   antik   antique

with ultimate care.

e. Bogart buzzed around the enormous

oke   oque   oak   tree.

f. Grit was disturbed by the

grotesque   grotesck

statue.

The /s/ sound is usually written as **s**, **ss** or **c**.
However, sometimes there is a silent **c** after the **s**, like in **scene**.
The /s/ sound spelled **sc** can be found at the beginning
or in the middle of words, but never at the end.

1 **Complete the table.**

Underline the letters that make the /s/ sound in each word in the box.
Then, write the words under the matching spelling pattern.

| scenic | assembly | sandal | scent | fascinating |
| decent | sensitive | muscle | kiss | succulent |

s	ss	c	sc

2 **Complete these words.**

Remember, the /s/ sound can be spelled **s**, **ss** or **sc**.

a.

n.

.... ent

b.

n.

.... andal

c.

n.

ki ....

d.

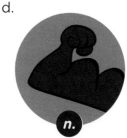

n.

mu .... le

3 Complete these sentences.

Choose the correct spelling below and fill in the blanks.

mussly / muscly	ascembly / assembly	succulent / scucculent
fascinating / fasinating	senic / scenic	sensitive / scensitive

a. Bearnice was __sensitive__ about her poor cookery skills.

b. Oz found the science of air travel _____ .

c. Grit stuffed several mangoes up his sleeves to make himself look really _____ .

d. The morning _____ went on for three hours.

e. Yang's jaw dropped when she saw the _____ dinner on the table.

f. Shang High and Yang took the longer, more _____ route.

Adverbs **describe verbs**. Remember,
a verb is a doing or being word.
Adverbs describe **how** or **when** we do things.

You can turn some adjectives into adverbs
by adding -**ly** to the end of them:

innocent + ly ➡ innocently

If the adjective ends in a -**y**,
like **happy**, you first have to remove
the -**y** and add an -**i** before adding -**ly**:

happy + i + ly ➡ happily

If the adjective ends in -**le**, like **simple**,
you remove the -**le** and add -**ly**:

simple + ly ➡ simply

If the adjective ends in -**ic**,
like **dramatic**, you add -**ally** instead:

dramatic + ally ➡ dramatically

1 Rewrite these sentences using adverbs.

The words in bold describe the action of the verb. Turn them into adverbs using the rules on the opposite page. The first one is done for you.

a. Armie forgot his lines **in a comical way**.

Armie forgot his lines comically.

b. Grit charged at the dragon **in a noble way**.

c. Shang High composed his latest song **in a frantic way**.

d. Oz cried all afternoon **in a tragic way**.

e. Yin picked the flowers **in a gentle way**.

f. Brick performed the experiment

in a meticulous way.

Suffixes are letters or groups of letters that are
added to the end of words to change their meaning.

Before you add a suffix to some words,
you have to first **double the final consonant**.

We know when to do this depending on whether there is
a **short or long vowel sound** before the **final consonant**.

When a root word ends in a **long vowel sound** followed
by a **consonant**, you **do not** need to double the final
consonant before adding **-ing**, **-ed**, **-er** or **-est**.

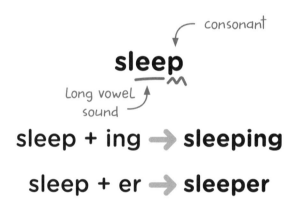

sleep + ing → **sleeping**

sleep + er → **sleeper**

When a root word ends in a **short vowel sound** followed
by a **consonant**, you need to **double the last letter**
first before adding **-ing**, **-ed**, **-er** or **-est**.

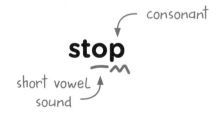

stop + p + ing → **stopping**

stop + p + ed → **stopped**

1 **Circle the words that are spelled correctly.**

dripped shoping nodding hopped

begging bigest swimer jogging

2 **Add the suffix -ing to the words below.**
Watch out for words ending in a short vowel sound followed
by a consonant.

a. trim → ....

b. slam → ....

c. jump → ....

d. seek → ....

e. forget → ....

f. toast → ....

3 **Add the suffixes -er and -est to the words below.**
Remember to double the last letter before adding the suffixes if the
root word ends in a short vowel followed by a consonant.

a. big → .... → ....

b. cheap → .... → ....

c. slim → .... → ....

d. hot → .... → ....

e. thin → .... → ....

f. young → .... → ....

4 **Circle the words that are spelled correctly in this story.**

The opening night of Plato's food truck had arguably been a huge success. The customers had loved his food and **tipped** **tiped** him generously. He had even been **crownned** **crowned** the **winner** **winer** of the Best Food Truck Award. However, Plato **regretted** **regreted** everything as he **listenned** **listened** to the morning radio.

"Hundreds of people have stomach aches after **eatting** **eating** at Plato's famous food truck last night. Plato boasted about **cookking** **cooking** with the **hottest** **hotest** chillies in the world, but those chillies clearly did not agree with the customers," announced the radio news reporter.

Plato **sighhed** **sighed** deeply. "Back to the drawing board," he thought to himself.

5 Now it's your turn!

Write three sentences using any of the following words with the suffixes **-ing**, **-ed**, **-er** or **-est**. Watch out! Not every suffix goes with every root word.

nap	**swap**	**sad**
flip	**flat**	**dim**

....

....

....

....

....

....

....

....

....

....

The suffix -**ation** can be added to some verbs to form a noun.

For some verbs, you just add -**ation**:

inform + ation ➔ information

For verbs that **end in -e**,
you usually **remove the final -e**
before adding **-ation**:

admir~~e~~ + ation ➔ admiration

For verbs that **end in -ate**,
you usually **remove the final -ate**
before adding **-ation**:

vibr~~ate~~ + ation ➔ vibration

TIP!

Understanding how words are connected helps to develop our word consciousness.
This is our awareness of words that helps us to spell and learn new vocabulary.

① Complete this story.
Transform these verbs into nouns by adding -**ation**.
Don't forget to watch out for words ending in -**e** or -**ate**.

Bearnice cares about all environmental issues. She loves recycling

and has a deep **(adore)** .... adoration .... for renewable energy.

Whenever she can, Bearnice gives her pocket money as a

(donate) .... to an environmental charity. So, it

was a huge honour when that environmental charity asked

Bearnice to be their spokesperson.

They were incredibly impressed by her commitment and

(determine) .... Bearnice needed very little

(prepare) .... for her first speech

on green energy because she had been practising it in the mirror

for years.

As she stepped up to the podium to deliver her speech, she felt the

tingling **(sense)** .... of pride. She knew that

together they could make a difference.

The suffix -**ous** can be added to some nouns
to turn them into adjectives. It means **full of**.

For some nouns, you just add -**ous**:

joy + ous → joyous

For most nouns that end in -**e**, you usually
remove the final -e before adding -**ous**:

nerve + ous → nervous

For nouns that end in a soft **g** sound (like in **g**iraffe)
followed by -**e**, you just add -**ous**:

outrage + ous → outrageous

For nouns that end in -**our**, you usually **replace
the -our with -or** before adding -**ous**:

glamour + or + ous → glamorous

1 Turn these nouns into adjectives.

Add the suffix -**ous** to these nouns to turn them into adjectives.
Remember to remove the final -**e** (unless it's a -**ge**) or replace
the -**our** with -**or** before adding -**ous**.

a. joy   → ....

b. humour   → ....

c. synonym   → ....

d. advantage → ....

e. rigour   → ....

② Complete this story.

Transform these nouns into adjectives by adding -**ous**.
Don't forget to watch out for words ending in -**e** or -**our**.

Yesterday, Yin and Yang decided to become **(fame)**

.... explorers. They wanted to be applauded

for their **(courage)** .... decision to explore the

Amazon rainforest in South America. This trip would be incredibly

(danger) .... because of all the **(poison)**

.... snakes that live there.

The twins knew it would take **(vigour)** ....

training to prepare them for this trip.

Some suffixes sound similar but are spelled differently, like -**sure** and -**ture**.

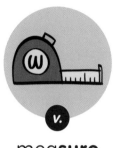

v.

mea**sure**

n.

pic**ture**

These suffixes sound similar but if you really pronounce them, you can tell the difference.

The -**sure** in treasure sounds like:

zhuh

The -**ture** in nature sounds like:

chuh

WATCH OUT!

Some words ending in the "chuh" sound aren't written –ture. If the root word already ends in –ch, then the suffix is simply –er. For example, teacher.

1 Complete these words.

Fill in the missing letters using the correct -**sure** or -**ture** spelling for each word. Remember to say the word out loud to hear if it has the **zhuh** (-**sure**) or **chuh** (-**ture**) sound.

a. enclo ....

b. struc ....

c. depar ....

d. plea ....

e. signa ....

f. sculp ....

2 Complete the news report below.

Fill in the gaps using the words you completed in activity 1.

At 4pm yesterday, fourteen gorillas escaped from their

.... at the zoo. Shortly after, the cunning

zookeepers devised a plan to lure the gorillas back. They built an

eight-metre-tall .... of Bonza, the head gorilla,

made entirely out of bananas. However, the ....

of this statue was very weak as bananas are a soft fruit, so it

collapsed an hour after being built.

"The gorillas brought a lot of ....

to visitors of this zoo. People queued for

hours to get a photograph or even a

messy .... from Bonza,

the world's first celebrity gorilla,"

commented a disheartened zookeeper.

Rumour has it that the gorillas were last seen boarding a

boat to Uganda, disguised as human passengers. Their

.... is a great loss to the zoo, but we at

Wordsmith Weekly are very pleased they've taken the

initiative to return to their natural habitat.

Some words are a little trickier to spell than others.
These words don't follow the rules we expect them to follow.

Some people call these exception words. We call them **rebel words**.

These are words we have to learn by heart
and it can be fun to practise them in different ways.

① Copy out these rebel words.

Underline the tricky parts of these spellings. Copy out each rebel word
twice and read it aloud. Extra challenge! Try not to look at the original
word the second time you write it out.

a.

n.

library

....

....

b.

adj.

disastrous

....

....

c.

n.

exercise

....

....

d.

n.

medicine

....

....

e.

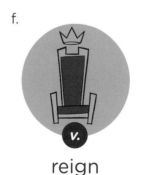

n.

restaurant

....

....

f.

v.

reign

....

....

g.

n.

potatoes

....

....

h.

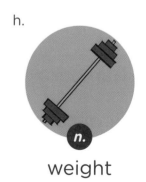

n.

weight

....

....

2 Complete the sentences.

Choose the correct spelling and fill in the blanks.

a. Yin and Yang swapped identities and the result was

....

disasterous   disastrous

b. Plato's .... closed after a chilli powder explosion.

restaurant   restrant

c. Brick does 100 press-ups as a warm-up before he starts his

....

exercise   exersize

d. It's much easier to lift .... on the moon because

waits   weights

there is less gravity.

e. Bearnice invented a .... that can cure

medisin   medicine

any disease.

f. Armie's favourite place in the world is the ....

library   libry

g. The king .... over the city for forty years.

rayned   reigned

h. Plato loved every form of cooked ....

potatoes   potatos

READING AND WRITING

Here, you will read character-rich fiction texts and illuminating non-fiction texts. You will answer some questions about the text and some questions that ask you to practise skills that you learned in the rest of the book. At the end of this section, there are prompts to help you take your writing to the next level.

In this section, we're going to focus on reading comprehension skills when reading fiction texts. Reading comprehension is all about reading a text carefully, taking your time and understanding it.

Here, we'll be reading the Mrs Wordsmith version of an **Ancient Greek myth**.

Myths are stories that were created by ancient cultures to make the natural world less of a scary place. The Ancient Greeks created myths that were tied to their religion and they often involved gods and goddesses as main characters.

You can identify myths by the way they involve courageous heroes, magical powers and fictional creatures like three-headed dogs.

Like fables and folktales, myths belong to the **oral tradition** of storytelling. This means that they were often passed on from generation to generation through the spoken word, instead of written down. The characters and the plot of each myth remained generally the same over time, but other details were added or taken away depending on the storyteller.

Before we read the Mrs Wordsmith retelling of the myth of **Theseus and the Minotaur**, let's take a look at some vocabulary.

intricate

adj. very complicated or detailed

--- WORD PAIRS ---

intricate **web**
intricate **machinery**
intricate **pattern**

labyrinth

n. a complex network of paths
that are difficult to escape

--- WORD PAIRS ---

complex labyrinth
vast labyrinth
underground labyrinth

tyrannical

adj. using your power to control
and harm others

--- WORD PAIRS ---

tyrannical **leader**
tyrannical **bully**
tyrannical **dictator**

voracious

adj. extremely hungry
or greedy

--- WORD PAIRS ---

voracious **monster**
voracious **reader**
voracious **appetite**

Theseus and the Minotaur

King Minos was a very powerful king who lived on the beautiful island of Crete. He was so powerful that people from all the surrounding kingdoms were afraid of him. He was such a bully that even his daughter, Ariadne, wasn't all that keen on him.

Like all rich and powerful kings, King Minos received an endless supply of rare and unusual gifts. He had an enormous golden statue of himself in his bedroom, he had a collection of ludicrously expensive togas and he had a pet peacock, to name a few. By far the most unusual gift that King Minos had ever been given, however, was the Minotaur, which he kept in an intricate, underground labyrinth.

The Minotaur was half man and half bull and survived on a strict diet of humans! In order to keep this Minotaur full, King Minos demanded that the people of Athens send seven men and seven women to Crete every year to be fed to the voracious monster. King Minos could get away with making these kinds of outrageous demands because everybody was so anxious to stay on his good side.

And so every year, fourteen unfortunate souls arrived from Athens and were released into the labyrinth, never to be seen again. Until one year, somebody decided to do something about this appalling situation. That somebody was Theseus. Theseus was the son of Aegeus, King of Athens, and he was big and strong and had nice hair. Theseus was sick and tired of King Minos' tyrannical behaviour and he didn't see why innocent Athenians should be sent to Crete and fed to a monster. The next time the dreaded day rolled around, Theseus volunteered himself to be sent to Crete.

When Theseus arrived in Crete and presented himself to King Minos, Ariadne (the king's daughter) fell head-over-heels in love with him. She was pleased that he planned to rid them of the Minotaur once and for all, but she was also sick with worry at the thought that Theseus might not make it out of the labyrinth alive. He had such beautiful hair!

"Even if you succeed in slaying the beast, how will you get out again?" she asked him. "The labyrinth always wins!"

"I'll be fine!" replied Theseus. "I'm extremely clever and wonderful!"

Ariadne, who was quite a lot more intelligent than Theseus, was not so sure. She was determined to find a way to save the gorgeous Athenian, so she stayed up all night coming up with a plan.

The next morning, as the crowds gathered to watch Theseus depart, Ariadne pulled him aside.

"Here is a ball of string," she whispered. "I will hold this end and you must unwind it as you go. Once you have destroyed the Minotaur, all you have to do is follow the string and it will bring you back to the entrance."

"Errrr... sure!" said Theseus, but the confused look on his face annoyed Ariadne.

Theseus was gone for ages and everybody held their breath. As time went on, people started shaking their heads and whispering in each other's ears. Ariadne found herself rapidly losing interest. If Theseus hadn't understood her beautifully simple plan, then it was his own fault!

Just as people started to make their way home, Theseus staggered out of the darkness holding Ariadne's string.

"Nobody eats Theseus for dinner..." he announced, and the crowd went wild. Ariadne rolled her eyes.

1 These statements are based on the instructions on page 128. Are they true or false?

True

False

a.

Myths are about real things that happened to real people.

b.

Myths involve magical elements that do not occur in real life.

c.

The details in myths are always the same in every version.

d.

Myths were usually written in books, which were passed down through generations.

2 Can you number these events in the order they happened in the story?

a. Theseus escapes the labyrinth.

b. Ariadne falls in love with Theseus.

c. King Minos receives a golden statue as a gift.

d. Ariadne feels annoyed with Theseus.

e. Theseus arrives on Crete.

3 Can you find a noun in the text that means the same as **maze**?

....

TIP!

If you aren't sure what a word means, go back to the text and use the context to help you work out the answer.

4 Draw lines connecting each of these words from the text to the correct synonym.

intricate	worried
anxious	very bad
unfortunate	unlucky
appalling	complicated

5 Illustrations tell us more about a character or setting. How does the first illustration of Theseus help to create a sense of who he is as a character?

....

....

....

6 Can you match these phrases
from the text with their meanings?

"everybody held their breath"	○ ○	the crowd were happy and made lots of noise
"the crowd went wild"	○ ○	nobody ever escapes from the labyrinth
"the labyrinth always wins"	○ ○	everybody waited nervously

7 What do you think Theseus thinks of Ariadne's plan
when she first tells him? Explain in your own words.

....

....

....

8 In this story, Ariadne's plan saves Theseus from the
labyrinth. So, why do you think Ariadne rolls her
eyes at the end of our Mrs Wordsmith version?

....

....

....

....

In this section, we'll be reading a screenplay about Bearnice and Brick in space. A screenplay is a kind of **script** that is written for **film or TV**. A script is a story that is written to be performed.

Scripts use **dialogue** and **stage directions** and tell the performers **how to say their lines**. Because screenplays are written for TV and film, these scripts also include information about **what the viewer will be able to see on screen**, including information about whether the scene is happening inside (INT.) or outside (EXT.) and whether it is day or night. You will often see the phrase **CUT TO** in screenplays. This tells us that the camera angle has changed or moved to a different **scene**, **location**, **time** or **character**.

1

First, you're going to read the opening from a **screenplay**. Take your time and read it carefully.

2

Then, use the text to help you answer the questions. If you aren't sure about an answer, go back and read the text again. All the information you need is in the text.

'In a Galaxy Nearby' – The Movie

CAST

Bearnice is an intrepid astronaut. She is the captain of her spaceship and it's her job to make sure the ship and everyone on it is safe.

Brick is Bearnice's second in command. It's Brick's job to control the spaceship from inside the control room and to obey all orders from the captain.

OPENING (INT.): THE INSIDE OF A SPACESHIP – ARTIFICIAL LIGHTING

We watch Bearnice zip up her spacesuit and open the latch on the spaceship wall. In the background behind her, we see outer space and Earth floating in the distance. Bearnice floats out into space.

***

CUT TO (EXT.): THE OUTSIDE OF A SPACESHIP – NIGHT

Bearnice is floating beside the spaceship door, which is shut. She uses her hands to pull herself along the side of the spaceship and inspects it as she goes.

BRICK
(his voice out of Bearnice's walkie-talkie)

This is Brick to Bearnice. Can you hear me, Captain? Over.

CAPTAIN BEARNICE

I can hear you. I have attached myself to the outside of the spaceship using the extra-strong cable and I am proceeding to check the external surfaces for signs of a collision. Over.

BRICK
(his voice out of Bearnice's walkie-talkie)

Very good, Captain. The computer indicates that the damage to the spaceship is on one of the wings. Over.

There is a tense silence as Bearnice makes her way slowly around the spaceship towards the wing.

CUT TO (INT.): THE SPACESHIP CONTROL ROOM – ARTIFICIAL LIGHTING

We see Brick sitting at the controls. He is silent and hyper-focused on various flashing lights and meters. Occasionally, he makes some minor adjustments to the controls.

CAPTAIN BEARNICE
(her voice over the radio)

I may have found something out here. Over.

BRICK

Describe it, Captain. Over.

CAPTAIN BEARNICE
(her voice over the radio)

It's hard to... It could be some kind of space junk. Although...

At this point, the sound starts to break up. We see a bead of sweat roll down Brick's forehead when his radio loses contact with Bearnice.

BRICK

Yes? Captain? Although what? Captain, can you hear me? Over.

CAPTAIN BEARNICE
(her voice over the radio)

Th-... whe- ... Some kind of... Horrible... Tu-... Gla-... You?

BRICK
(urgently)

I can't understand anything, Captain. Get back inside! Over.

1 Which of these features can be found in this screenplay?

Put a tick next to all the correct answers.

a. information about what kind of light there is ◯

b. information about background music ◯

c. information about what can be seen on camera ◯

d. character names to tell you who is speaking ◯

2 What is Captain Bearnice doing in this opening extract?

Underline the correct answer.

a. She is giving the outside of the spaceship a much needed scrub.

b. She is looking for aliens.

c. She is looking for damage on the outside of the spaceship.

3 Find and copy one detail from the script that shows us that Brick is worried.

....

....

....

....

....

4 How would you describe the atmosphere
of this scene? Give evidence of your answer.

....

....

....

....

....

....

5 Can you explain why the ending of this extract
is a cliffhanger?

....

....

....

....

....

....

....

....

....

In this section, we're going to focus on reading comprehension skills when reading non-fiction texts. Reading comprehension is all about reading a text carefully, taking your time and understanding it.

First, you're going to read a **news article** about **access to education**. Take your time and read the article slowly.

Then, use the text to help you answer the questions. If you aren't sure about an answer, go back and read the article again. All the information you need is in the text.

VOCABULARY

campaign

v. **to work in an organised way towards a specific goal**
The pupils campaigned to increase recycling in their school.

dismay

v. **to make someone feel unhappy and disappointed**
The director was dismayed when all her actors forgot their lines.

impairment

n. **a loss of function of a body part as a result of an injury, disease or medical condition**
The student has a hearing impairment so uses a hearing aid to help her communicate.

braille

n. **a written language for visually impaired people with each letter represented by patterns of raised dots**
The latest action thriller novel is available in braille.

Wordsmith Weekly

Vol. 132   30 SEPTEMBER   £3.00

ONE PUPIL'S FEARLESS CAMPAIGN FOR ACCESS TO EDUCATION

Bronze Oak Primary School has been educating children aged four to eleven for over seventy years. It is a school beloved by hundreds of pupils and Lila campaigned for the right to be one of them.

Lila, aged eight, was dismayed to find out that she would be unable to attend Bronze Oak because of the school's lack of resources to accommodate a visually impaired pupil. Visual impairment is used to describe any kind of vision loss, ranging from someone who cannot see at all to someone who has partial vision loss. Lila has amblyopia, a condition where vision does not develop properly in childhood. Amblyopia is caused by one or both eyes being unable to build a strong link to the brain.

This usually only affects one eye and it is estimated that 1 in 50 children develop this condition.

The following is an extract from a series of letters Lila sent to the school's board of governors, headteacher and staff: "My brother loves Bronze Oak Primary School. He says it is an amazing place to learn new things and meet lots of new friends. I think I should have the same opportunity."

Lila argued that if education is a human right, then it should be accessible for all. Human rights are the basic rights and freedoms all people are entitled to. They include issues like the right to life, security, expression and education.

Lila campaigned for technology and adapted learning materials, such as large print or braille, to help her and other visually impaired students access their school work. After her meeting with Bronze Oak's special educational needs co-ordinator, the school is striving to ensure that Lila and other children with visual impairments are given the opportunity to thrive at Bronze Oak.

The school's headteacher stated, "Usually in schools, it's teachers that are asking pupils to learn and adapt, but in this situation Lila turned the tables and asked us."

Accessibility for visually impaired pupils marks a new era for Bronze Oak Primary School, with Lila at the forefront of the campaign. Both pupils and staff understand that this is only the beginning. 1.8 million pupils in England have Special Educational Needs (SEN) and there is so much more schools can do to support these students. Multi-sensory learning, such as audio and hands-on activities, can improve accessibility for all pupils. Lila is now campaigning for other schools to follow in Bronze Oak's footsteps.

1 **What was Lila campaigning for?**

....

....

....

....

....

....

2 "One Pupil's Fearless
Campaign for Access to Education"
Why do you think the article's title describes
Lila's campaign with the adjective **fearless**?

....

....

....

....

3 What is amblyopia caused by?

....

....

4 Who does Lila know that already
attends Bronze Oak Primary School?

....

5 Who did Lila send letters to?

....

6 What are **human rights**?

....

7 What does SEN stand for?

....

8 **What does the phrase turned the tables mean?**

The school's headteacher explained, "Usually in schools, it's teachers that are asking pupils to learn and adapt, but in this situation Lila turned the tables and asked us."

....

....

....

9 **Circle the words that are synonyms of thrive.**

"... to ensure that Lila and other children with visual impairments are given the opportunity to thrive at Bronze Oak."

fail   succeed   survive

flourish   socialise   entertain

10 **Explain why it is so important to accommodate all pupils in schools.**

....

....

....

....

....

11 **Lila felt strongly about something.**
What is something you feel strongly about?

This could be anything from more recycling bins at school
to demanding a water park be opened in your back garden.

....

....

12 **Lila wrote a letter fighting for the thing**
she felt strongly about. Can you write
a letter to someone arguing for your belief?

Time to write!

It could be a teacher, a politician or just a friend who you think
might be interested. This type of writing is sometimes called
an opinion piece. Support your point of view with a list of reasons
and think about the following questions: Who are you writing to?
Why should they help you? What actions do they need to take?

....

....

....

....

....

....

....

....

....

....

1

First, you're going to read a **persuasive text**.
Take your time and read the text slowly.

2

Then, use the text to help you answer the questions.
If you aren't sure about an answer, go back and read
the text again. All the information you need is in the text.

The main purpose of a **persuasive text**
is to present a point of view and persuade
the reader to agree.

A **persuasive text** could be a letter to your
headteacher asking for a longer lunch break,
an article promoting recycling, a strongly worded
movie review or even an **advertisement**.

An **advertisement** (sometimes shortened to an advert)
is something that often tries to persuade someone
to buy a product or service.

DID YOU KNOW?

Persuade means to make someone
do or believe something through
reasoning or argument.

HOW DO ADVERTS PERSUADE?

Positive language

Adverts will often use positive and exaggerated language to promote their product. This includes words like **bestselling**, **healthiest** and **exclusive**.

Promises

To convince you the product is worth it, adverts will make lots of promises, like **this product will change your life** or **this product will solve all your problems!** Some of these promises might be in the form of **positive reviews**.

Standing out

To grab your attention, adverts will use **humour**, **questions** and **word play** including **slogans**, **rhyme**, **alliteration** and much more.

DID YOU KNOW?

Alliteration is using the same sound at the beginning of several words that are close together in a sentence, for example, perfectly persuasive product posters!

DREAM RECORDER 3000

Where all your dreams come true

Have you ever woken up from an incredible, life-changing dream... only to forget what it was about a few seconds later? You remember bits and pieces, like it was set in space, your aunt was there and you think there was probably an alien egg-and-spoon race involved. Despite how memorable all that sounds, you can't quite put your finger on exactly what happened.

Well, those days are over. Never forget a dream again with the **DREAM RECORDER 3000**! Download our app, plug yourself in and rest easy knowing that all your dreams will be ready to watch in high definition when you wake up.

Whether you dream about dangerous dragons, detestable dentists or disco dancing... this product is for you!

From the makers of **DAYDREAM IN VIDEO GAMES** and **ANIMATE YOUR AFTERNOON NAP**, SleepTech Incorporated uses cutting-edge technology to record your dreams.

"It changed my life!"

Bearnice

☆☆☆☆☆

"It inspired me to make my dreams come true!"

Plato

☆☆☆☆☆

"I've filled up fourteen dream journals so far!"

Oz

☆☆☆☆☆

"This is the #1 Dream Recorder in the world."

Professor of Dream Technology

☆☆☆☆☆

THE DREAM RECORDER IS READY TO ORDER!

BUY NOW! SELLING FAST!

1 **What promise does this advert make?**

....

....

2 **What does the phrase cutting-edge technology mean?**
Tick your answer.

a. Old technology   ◯

b. New technology   ◯

c. Cheap technology   ◯

3 **What are the two other products made by SleepTech Incorporated?**

....

....

4 **Who said this quote?**
"I've filled up fourteen dream journals so far!"

....

5 **Copy out the sentence that uses alliteration.**

....

....

....

6 **Can you name two persuasive devices used in this advert?**
Give short quotes to show each one.

....

....

....

....

....

7 **Which piece of information in the text would be most likely to persuade you to buy the DREAM RECORDER 3000?**
Circle the information in the text and explain why here.

....

....

....

8 **Now it's your turn!**
Write two sentences to advertise the fictional product
SUPERGUM, a chewing gum with over a million flavours.
Make sure to stand out using positive language and promises.
As an extra challenge, try to include alliteration or rhyme.

Time to write!

....

....

....

....

First, you're going to read an **explanation text** about **drones**.
Take your time and read the text slowly.

Then, use the text to help you answer the questions.
If you aren't sure about an answer, go back and read the article again.
All the information you need is in the text.

DID YOU KNOW?

Explanation texts help you understand how things work.

VOCABULARY

conservationist

n. **someone who works to preserve
and protect the environment and wildlife**
The wildlife conservationist worked
tirelessly to save the rainforest.

endangered

adj. **at risk of dying out completely**
The species of rhino was so endangered
that there was only one of them left.

rotor

n. **a part of a machine that spins,
often used as the device supporting
the turning blades of a helicopter**
The rotor spluttered to life and began to spin,
causing the helicopter to begin hovering.

thrust

n. **the force produced by an engine
that pushes in a specific direction**

The thrust of the engines caused
the rocket to launch into space.

gravitational force

n. **the force by which all objects
in the universe are attracted to each other**

On Earth, objects fall to the ground
because of a strong gravitational force.

'Drone' is the common name for
an unmanned aerial vehicle (UAV).
This is an aircraft without a pilot,
crew or passengers on board.
Drones are operated remotely
and can hover and fly in all directions.
They can vary dramatically in quality,
cost and size, with the largest drone
being 24 metres long and the smallest
being 4 centimetres long.

Drones have many different uses
to many different groups of people.
Filmmakers use drones to get the perfect
aerial shot of a fast-moving car chase.
Wildlife conservationists use drones to
observe the habits of an endangered
species without disturbing them.
Farmers use drones to plan water flow
management and plant seeds in their fields.

How do drones fly?

Drones use rotors to fly. Helicopters are usually flown by a pilot and have one rotor. As drones are unmanned, they need more stability than helicopters so they usually have four rotors.

Rotors are like fans. When the blades of a rotor start spinning, they push air down. At the same time, air pushes up on the rotor. This is the force which makes the drone move and is called the rotor's thrust. This is how the drone is able to hover, ascend and descend.

1

Hovering

To hover, the **thrust** of the four rotors pushing the drone up must be <u>equal to</u> the **gravitational force** pulling it down. Then, the drone can stay in place in the air.

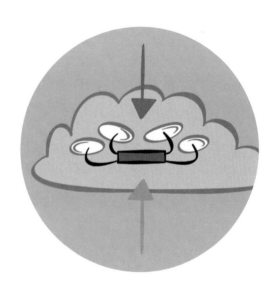

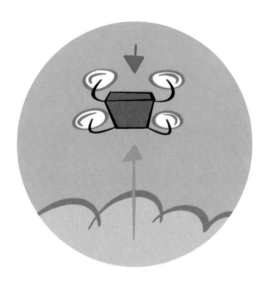

2

Ascending

To ascend, the **thrust** of the four rotors pushing the drone up must be <u>greater than</u> the **gravitational force** pulling it down.

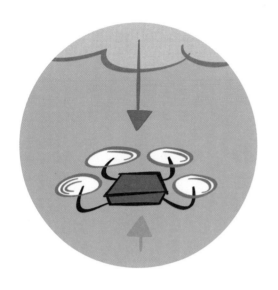

3

Descending

To descend, the **thrust** of the four rotors pushing the drone up must be less than the **gravitational force** pulling it down.

 gravitational force

thrust

Drones can be used to transport all sorts of items, but these items make the drone heavier and so increase the gravitational force pulling it down. With enough thrust, a drone can carry heavier and heavier items. With enough thrust, a drone can be used to carry a person!

1 **What does UAV stand for?**

Circle the correct answer.

> underwater
> aerial vehicle

> unmanned
> aerial vehicle

> unmanned
> aeroplane vehicle

> unmanned
> aerial vacuum

2 **Name three groups of people who might use drones.**

....

....

....

3 **Choose one group from the previous question and explain what they use drones for.**

....

....

....

4 **What does the word hover mean?**

....

5 **What machine are rotors likened to in the text?**

....

6 Match the statement to the action it would cause.

a. The rotors' thrust is **equal to** the gravitational force.

b. The rotors' thrust is **less than** the gravitational force.

c. The rotors' thrust is **greater than** the gravitational force.

ascend

hover

descend

7 Explain why this statement is incorrect using information in the text.

"The heavier an item, the **less** thrust needed to carry it with a drone."

A **simile** is a writing device that compares one thing to something else in a way that makes it easier for a reader to imagine. Writers use them to make their descriptions more vivid.

Similes are usually used to make writing more interesting or exciting, so they often include exaggeration.

The giraffe was **as** tall **as** a skyscraper.

The elephant's legs were **like** tree trunks.

TIP!

Similes always include the words as or like.

1 Complete these similes!

Use your imagination to finish these similes. Remember, the best similes compare two things that are alike, like candy floss and clouds or snowflakes and glitter.

a. Woah! That lizard is as fast as ....

b. This stew tastes like ....

c. The movie was as .... as ....

d. Did you know that your breath smells like ....?

e. My pet goldfish is as .... as ....

A **metaphor** is a writing device that describes one thing as if it were another thing. This is done to make writing more interesting and to help the reader imagine complex concepts easily.

The judge's heart was made of stone.

The judge's heart was not actually made of stone. That is just the **literal meaning**. A literal meaning is when each word in a phrase stays true to its actual meaning.

Describing the judge's heart as made of stone implies that it was cold, hard and unfeeling. This meaning is figurative. A **figurative meaning** is when the combination of words in a phrase means more than just the most obvious interpretation.

1 **Match the metaphor to its meaning.**

a. My bedroom was a pigsty.　　　　It has soft and white fur.

b. She is a walking dictionary.　　　　It has ups and downs.

c. The cat was a fluffy cloud.　　　　It was messy.

d. Life is a roller coaster.　　　　She knows lots of words.

Now it's time to apply everything you've learned so far and get writing! In this section, you will write **a short story** based on a writing prompt.

When it's finished, this story will have four paragraphs: **an opening**, **a build-up**, **a climax** and **a resolution**.

This is sometimes called a **story mountain** because of how the plot builds up and then comes down when a resolution is found.

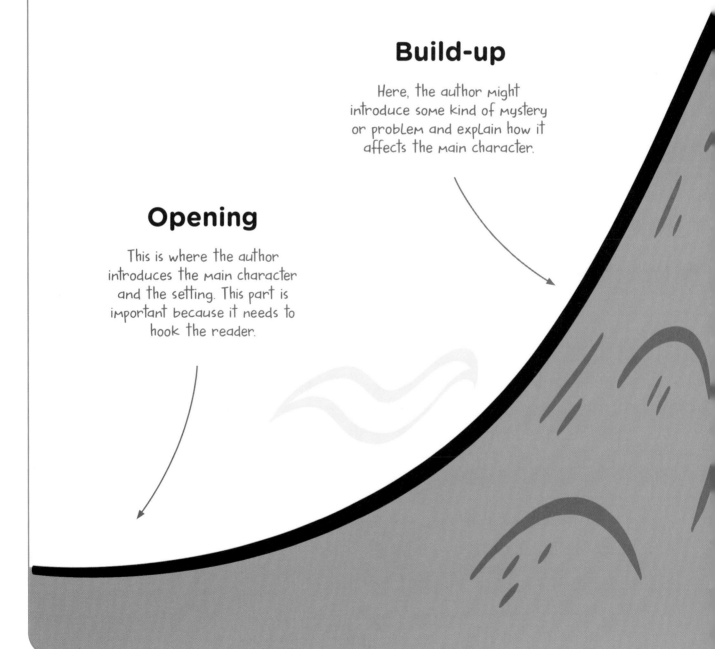

Build-up

Here, the author might introduce some kind of mystery or problem and explain how it affects the main character.

Opening

This is where the author introduces the main character and the setting. This part is important because it needs to hook the reader.

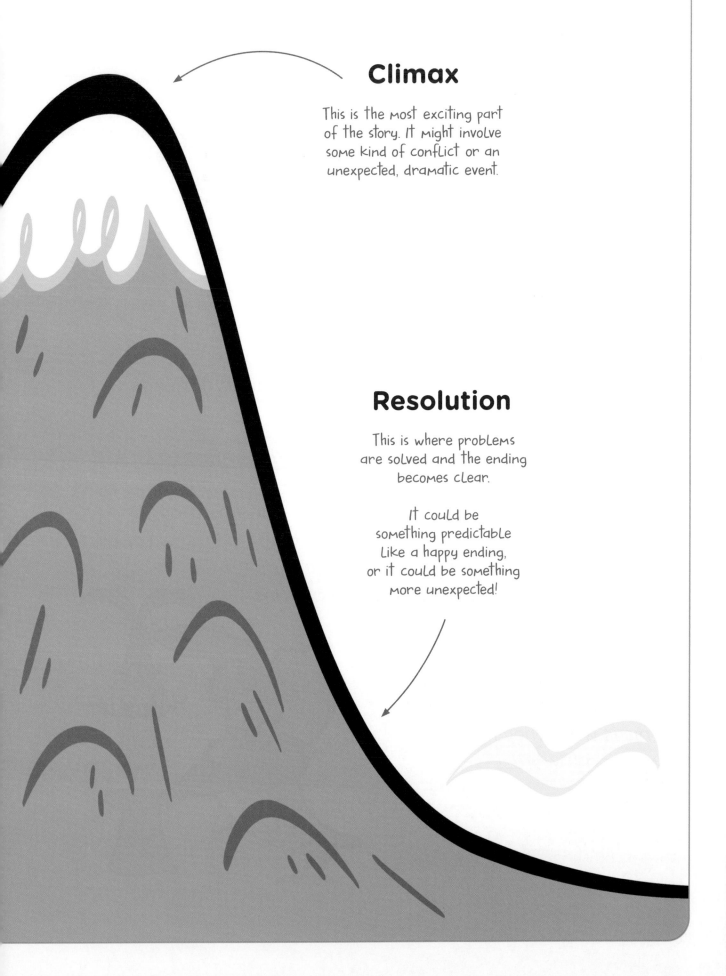

Climax

This is the most exciting part
of the story. It might involve
some kind of conflict or an
unexpected, dramatic event.

Resolution

This is where problems
are solved and the ending
becomes clear.

It could be
something predictable
like a happy ending,
or it could be something
more unexpected!

Your first prompt is to write about

two friends entering a talent show

The first paragraph (the **opening**) is written for you. It is your job to write the next three paragraphs (the **build-up**, the **climax** and the **resolution**).

Opening

This is where the author introduces the main characters and the setting. This part is important because it needs to hook the reader. Here, we introduced the two friends and the talent show.

Brick and Armie were unlikely friends. Brick was a tall, confident fitness-fanatic and Armie was small, shy and loved to read. On the surface, it seemed as though the duo had nothing in common... Nothing, that is, except for a love of magic. Ever since they first met, Brick and Armie had been working on their double act called The Magnificent Magicians. When they saw an advert for a local talent show, they knew they had to enter. This is what they had been working towards!

1 Build-up

Now it's your turn! This is where you introduce some kind of mystery or problem and explain how it affects the main character. This problem will be Brick feeling nervous. In this paragraph, you will describe Brick and Armie's preparation for the talent show and Brick's experiences of feeling more and more nervous. To help you write this paragraph, here are some writing goals:

TIP!

Use similes and metaphors in your writing to bring your descriptions alive for your reader.

a. Use a sentence that consists of two clauses joined by a coordinating conjunction, like **and**, **or** or **but**.

b. Show how the characters are feeling through their actions and their dialogue.

2 Climax

This is the most exciting part of the story. Here, you will describe the moment that Brick's stage fright causes everything to go terribly wrong during their performance. To help you write this paragraph, here are some writing goals:

DID YOU KNOW?

Stage fright is the anxiety or fear that occurs when performing on stage in front of lots of people. It can happen to anyone!

a. Use fronted adverbials of time to speed up the pace of your writing, like **suddenly** or **as quick as a flash**.

b. Use punctuation to make your writing more dramatic, such as exclamation marks and ellipses.

③ Resolution

This is where problems are solved and the ending becomes clear. Here, you will need to describe the moment Armie helps Brick overcome his fears and they win the talent show! To help you write this paragraph, here are some writing goals:

a. Use direct speech with inverted commas, like **"Thank you for watching," said Armie** or **Armie said, "Thank you for watching."**

b. Use an idiom (a phrase with a non-literal meaning), like **piece of cake** (meaning easy) or **on cloud nine** (meaning very happy).

....

....

....

....

....

....

....

....

....

....

....

....

....

Your next prompt is to write about

someone who picks up the wrong suitcase at the airport

The first paragraph (the **opening**) is written for you. It is your job to write the next three paragraphs (the **build-up**, the **climax** and the **resolution**).

Opening

This is where the author introduces the main characters and the setting. This part is important because it needs to hook the reader.

As Bearnice's flight home landed at the airport, she reminisced about the incredible trip she was returning from. She had spent the last ten days exploring the Amazon rainforest, taking wildlife surveys and collecting samples of rare plants that could be used for various scientific experiments. She had secured all her samples in a large, red suitcase and checked her baggage in before the flight. Bearnice smiled to herself as she waited by the conveyor belt for her important luggage to arrive.

1 Build-up

Now it's your turn! This is where you introduce some kind of mystery or problem and explain how it affects the main character. Here, you will describe how and why Bearnice accidentally collects the wrong piece of luggage and takes it with her to the laboratory. To help you write this paragraph, here are some writing goals:

a. Use at least three adverbs (words that describe verbs) to add descriptive details, like **safely**, **hopelessly** or **hungrily**.

b. Include at least two complex sentences with a main clause and subordinate clause. Remember, some common subordinating conjunctions that link a subordinate clause to a main clause are: **because**, **when**, **as**, **after** and **until**.

....

....

....

....

....

....

....

....

....

....

....

2 Climax

This is the most exciting part of the story. Here, you will describe the moment Bearnice realises she has the wrong luggage. What is inside? How does she feel? To help you write this paragraph, here are some writing goals:

a. Start your paragraph with a fronted adverbial phrase to establish the new place or time that the events were happening, like **later that day** or **at the bus stop**.

b. Use direct questions or exclamation sentences to make your writing more exciting, like **"What could she do?"** or **"What a dreadful situation it was!"**

③ Resolution

This is where problems are resolved and the story is concluded. Here, you will need to describe how Bearnice's suitcase is returned to her. Is there a surprising twist? Is there a lucky coincidence? To help you write this paragraph, here are some writing goals:

a. Use at least three adjectives (words that describe nouns) to add descriptive detail, like **mammoth**, **intimidating** or **determined**.

b. Conclude the story with a summary sentence. As an extra challenge, try to refer back to a detail in the first paragraph.

Now that you've written your own stories,
you're more than ready to edit someone else's!

1 **First, read through this text.**

"I'm scared," admitted Shang High as he and Bearnice <u>steped</u>

further into the haunted house. <u>they</u> had always been curious

about the eerily empty house at

the end of their street and had

decided that today was

the day to investigate.

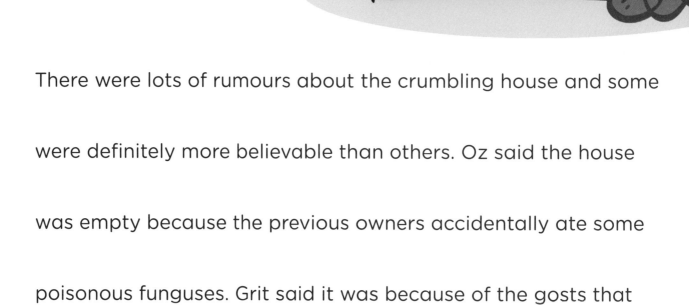

There were lots of rumours about the crumbling house and some

were definitely more believable than others. Oz said the house

was empty because the previous owners accidentally ate some

poisonous <u>funguses</u>. Grit said it was because of the <u>gosts</u> that lived in the attic and sang karaoke loudly every night. Bogart said

it was because the previous owners were turned into peanut

butter by a wicked witch. Shang High had avoided eating peanut

butter for weeks after hearing Bogarts theory, just in case.

"Follow I," whispered Bearnice as she began to climb the creaking

staircase. "Why are you going upstairs," hissed Shang High with

a shaky breath. Bearnice gave his a steely look and replied "We

need to find out what's going on here."

Until they had solved the mystery Bearnice was determind to keep

searching. Apprehensively Shang High followed.

2 Now, go back and correct the errors.

All the errors in this text have been underlined and it's your job to fix
them using skills that you learned in the rest of this book. The underlined
mistakes include spelling, punctuation and grammar errors.

3 Can you improve this story?

You've edited to make corrections, now let's try editing to improve a text. The rumours told by Oz, Grit and Bogart in paragraph two aren't nearly spooky enough.

Oz said the house was empty because the previous owners accidentally ate some poisonous funguses. Grit said it was because of the gosts that lived in the attic and sang karaoke loudly every night. Bogart said it was because the previous owners were turned into peanut butter by a wicked witch.

Can you rewrite them? Feel free to be as creative as you like and expand your ideas across more than one sentence.

Don't forget to use adjectives (words that describe nouns) and adverbs (words that describe verbs) to make your sentences more exciting.

So far in this chapter, we have done a lot of reading practice, but really the best reading practice is **reading for fun**!

Here are some tips for doing your best reading (and having a ridiculously good time while you're at it):

1

Create a cosy reading spot at home.
Reading time is you time and you deserve it.

2

Read often. Do it at the breakfast table,
do it before bed, do it on the toilet,
do it while you wait for the bus.

3

If you find yourself in a reading slump,
try re-reading your favourite book or reading
the book version of your favourite movie.

4

Shop around. Ask your friends and family what they
read for fun. You might be a huge fan of sci-fi, or books
about Antarctica, and not even know it yet. And remember,
not everything you read has to look the same. To get inspired,
let's find out what the Mrs Wordsmith characters like to read...

Yang

I tried reading fiction because everyone always bangs on about getting lost in the story, but it just wasn't for me... They're never funny enough. I like joke books, like, entire books that are just joke after joke after joke. What do librarians take with them when they go fishing? Bookworms! I could read that kind of thing forever and never get bored.

Cookbooks, baking books, books about the history of candy floss, autobiographies of famous chefs, *101 Things to do with Sherbet*, *Sushi: A Love Letter to Japanese Cookery*, *Around the World in 80 Sandwiches*... You get the picture. I like books about food.

PLato

The back of a cereal box. Trust me. The cereal companies are definitely trying to tell us something...

If I'm reading, then it's probably about sport. I get all the latest sports news online and that's how I stay on top of what every single player is doing. I'll start with the latest statistics over breakfast and then I'll sink into a tasty bit of commentary from my favourite pundits before bed. I do sometimes enjoy a drop of poetry when the mood takes me. My favourite is *Rhyme Stew* by Roald Dahl.

Shang High

Brick

I will read any genre as long as it's fiction! Anything that lets me escape into another world. I absolutely loved the detective series *High-Rise Mystery* by Sharna Jackson.

I'm reading *The Complete Illustrated Encyclopaedia of Freshwater Fish and Creatures* from start to finish. I found it in a pile of old books at a charity shop and it's blowing my mind. So far, I've memorised the names of 300 out of the 650 different species in the book. Salmon, chubs, crocodiles, eels, piranhas, catfish, kobudai... Test me! Did you know that the kobudai changes from female to male during its life?

Armie

Bearnice

1 **What would you recommend for someone else to read?**

Write down three of your favourite texts.

....

....

....

2 **Extra challenge!**

Ask three people what the best thing they've read this year is. Write down their answers here so you can remember to read them at some point!

....

....

....

....

....

....

Yin

DO NOT DISTURB

Page 10

1 a. common: television, days
b. common: girl
     proper: Morocco
c. common: library
     proper: Saturday, Armie
d. common: dog
     proper: Brazil
e. common: food
     proper: Tokyo
f. common: sculpture
     proper: Plato

2 Your answers might be something like:
common: chocolate, book, music
proper: Anna, Ali, London

Page 11

1 Your answers might be something like:
the famous actor with lots of fans
the piano with five keys missing
the extremely expensive shampoo

Pages 12–13

1 a. Brick was ravenous so he demolished
his lunch in thirty seconds.
b. Yin and Yang laughed joyfully as
they leaped up and down.

2 ... when **she** finished... **It** had been a
huge success... Brick because **he** was
jumping up and down... **She** couldn't
wait to go... because **they** had promised...

Pages 14–15

1 ... I invited **her** to the beach...
ate **it** by the water... filmed **them**
stealing... knocked **us** over...

2 a. them   **b.** him   **c.** her
d. it   **e.** us

Pages 16–17

1 a. That apple is mine.
b. That ball is his.
c. Those socks are theirs.
d. That hat is yours.

e. That shoe is hers.
f. Those seats are ours.

2 a. he   **b.** mine   **c.** her

Pages 18–19

1 a. The treasure chest, which nobody
had laid eyes on in 100 years,
was sticking out of the sand.
b. Oz opened the door for Bearnice,
who had brought fifty cupcakes
with her.
c. The ancient tree, which had been
standing there for many centuries,
fell to the ground.
d. Yin, who had never used a VR
headset before, was completely
immersed in the experience.

2 Your answers might be something like:
a. Bearnice, who was in a terrible
mood, was not impressed by the
fireworks.
b. The telephone, which nobody
answered, stopped ringing.
c. Plato knocked on the door of the
house, which had been abandoned
for ten years.
d. The slime, which was dripping from
the ceiling, had a horrible texture.

Page 20

1 a. laughed   **b.** strolled
c. wandered   **d.** crawled

2 a. I whisper   **b.** she sighs
c. he stumbles   **d.** you tiptoe

Page 21

1 tell – told
go – went
begin – began
give – gave
wear – wore
buy – bought

write – wrote
speak – spoke
think – thought

Pages 22–23

1 **a.** and finds a secret clue.
   b. and watches the sheep graze.
   c. because she broke her favourite pencil.
   d. but he loves blueberries even more!
   e. after he bought a new cookbook.
   f. and hoped some flowers would grow.

2 explore, buried, began, preserved, lived

Page 24

1 **a.** Bearnice is speaking
   (or she is speaking)
   b. Yin and Yang are baking
   (or they are baking)
   c. you are considering
   d. I am singing

2 **a.** Brick and Bogart were building
   (or they were building)
   b. I was expecting
   c. he was observing
   d. we were racing

Page 25

1 **a.** Shang High and Oz have relaxed all day.
   b. Armie has read lots of adventure books.
   c. They have carried the heavy bags for you.
   d. You have danced the tango.
   e. I have told funny stories.

Pages 26–27

1 **a.** must   **b.** might   **c.** should   **d.** can

2 **a.** Shang High   **b.** Yang   **c.** Oz

Pages 28–30

1 Your answers might be something like:
   a. eerie   **b.** sinister
   c. precipitous   **d.** ominous
   e. perilous   **f.** deafening

Page 31

1 Your answers might be something like:
   a. deafeningly   **b.** precipitously
   c. eerily   **d.** sinisterly
   e. ominously   **f.** perilously

Pages 32–33

1 after a while, far away, by the bank of the river, very bravely

2 **a.** as fast as she could
   b. Above the clouds
   c. There is no adverbial phrase here.
   d. in the blink of an eye
   e. over the edge of the cliff

3 **a.** Back at the train station,
   b. All of a sudden,
   c. with an intense passion

4 Your answers might be something like:
   a. Plato had made great progress by sunset.
   b. After a while, Bearnice gave up.

Pages 34–35

1 **a.** because a fly flew into his mouth
   b. when Yang told her secret
   c. When Grit felt sad

2 **a.** After waiting hours for the lift, Plato took the stairs.
   b. Oz loves going to the dentist because she gets a sticker.
   c. When it gets cold, Bearnice wears gloves and a scarf.

3 Your answers might be something like:
   a. Grit thought he had caught a gigantic fish when he felt something tug on the line.

  b. Yin ate a decadent slice of chocolate fudge cake after completing the marathon.

  c. When he saw his plan coming together, Bogart chuckled softly.

  d. Yang confidently skied down the mountain until one of her skis came off.

Pages 36–37

1 a. under   **b.** on   **c.** next to

2 a. under   **b.** after   **c.** beside
  d. above   **e.** outside **f.** on

Pages 38–39

1 a. and   **b.** and   **c.** but   **d.** or

2 Your answers might be something like:

  a. Armie visited the library every day but he had never been to the gardening section.

  b. Yang considered dyeing her fur blonde but she was scared of going to the hairdresser.

  c. Plato worked on the top floor of a skyscraper and he loved being high up in the clouds.

  d. Oz felt queasy after riding roller coasters all day but she was keen to return the next day to do it all again.

  e. Brick wanted to be a professional weightlifter or he wanted to be a ballet dancer.

  f. Shang High's ship was headed straight for an iceberg but he refused to accept that it was time to escape.

  g. Grit set off on a voyage around the world and he was feeling very excited.

Pages 40–41

1 a. when **b.** because   **c.** as **d.** after

2 Your answers might be something like:

  a. The bitter lemonade made Plato's eyes water because it was so sour.

  b. Bogart spilt beans everywhere when the doorbell rang.

  c. Shang High lost his lucky towel after he left it on the beach.

  d. Yin eats oats every morning for breakfast as they keep her full until lunch.

  e. A magical genie emerged from the lamp so Brick made a wish.

  f. Brick carried a heavy briefcase everywhere until he realised he could use a suitcase with wheels.

Pages 44–45

1 a. Bogart wants to take over the city, the country and the world.

  b. Yang built a sandcastle using a bucket, a spade and a lot of sand.

  c. Oz hates cabbage, mushrooms, olives and anchovies.

  d. The secret to building a robot is hard work, commitment and a little bit of luck.

  e. The baker whisked the eggs, sieved the flour and preheated the oven to 180 degrees.

2 a. Plato loved to cook breakfast, lunch and dinner.

  b. For her birthday, Oz wanted to go to a theme park, a seaside resort or a haunted house.

  c. The gardener planted seeds, watered the plants and cut the grass.

3 Your answer might be something like:
Shang High's stomach rumbled loudly as he looked over the spaghetti, potatoes, salad, guacamole, roast chicken, lasagne and chocolate cake.

Page 46

1 a. Because the fence is very tall, it is difficult to see into Bogart's garden.

  b. When there is lots of traffic, Armie likes to listen to the radio.

2 a. Until he won the lottery, Shang High lived in a very small cottage.

b. Until he found the perfect recipe, Plato would keep baking cakes.

Pages 47

1 a. In his secret lair, Bogart devised a cunning plan.

b. After hours of work, Grit finally perfected the wheel.

c. By midnight, Oz's phone had run out of battery.

2 Your answer might be something like:
After a day of struggling, Bogart was still tangled in the web.

Pages 48-49

1 a. "I'm sorry," whispered Yin.

b. "Where is the library?" asked Armie.

c. "Stop it!" yelled Oz.

d. Plato said, "This soup is too salty."

2 Your answers might be something like:

a. "I'm bored," grumbled Grit.

b. "Why are all ceilings so low?" asked Shang High.

c. "Let's take over the world!" screamed Bogart.

Pages 50-53

1 I would – I'd
what is – what's
I am – I'm
we are – we're
will not – won't
do not – don't
I will – I'll
should not – shouldn't

2 a. I'd love some whipped cream please!

b. "**Don't** move!" shouted the detective.

c. I'm very happy to see you!

d. "**We're** in this together!" Bearnice told Oz.

e. What's your favourite ice cream flavour?

f. Yang **shouldn't** have lied to Yin!

g. "I **won't** do this again," promised Bogart.

h. She's the first ostrich to win this award!

3 I'm > I am
don't > do not
didn't > did not
shouldn't > should not
I'd > I would

4 You **won't** believe what has happened. I know **we're** meant to... but **I'm** too upset... I think **I'll** stay at home.

Pages 54-55

1 a. Armie's pile of books.

b. the business' office

c. Bearnice's suitcase

d. the hairdressers' salon

e. the mice's cheese

f. the family's television

2 Your answer might be something like:
Shang High's lucky trainers were all he needed to win the race.

Page 56

1 a. It's   **b.** its   **c.** it's   **d.** its

2 a. It has never snowed in the summer before!

b. "It is my birthday tomorrow," sang Oz.

Pages 57

1 a. your   **b.** You're   **c.** your   **d.** You're
e. your   **f.** your   **g.** You're   **h.** your

Pages 58-59

1 a. "I can't remember..." replied Shang High.

b. All of a sudden, the aliens arrived...

2 Watermelons... are believed to have originated in Africa.

3 a. word or words have been removed

b. create suspense

c. trailing off

d. word or words have been removed

e. trailing off

4 Your answer might be something like:

a. I thought I could see something moving between the trees...

b. The door opened slowly, with a creak...

Pages 60–61

1 ... declared Brick.//Outside of the factory...

... with slimy scales.//One week later...

Pages 62–63

1 Penguin feet are adapted to walk long distances. – They have four toes, unlike the five typical of mammals.

Penguins are only found in the Southern Hemisphere. – The greatest concentrations are on the Antarctic coasts.

Penguins eat silverfish, krill and squid. – Adult penguins eat 2–3 kilograms of fish per day.

Penguins have black and white feathers. – These feathers are short and dense.

2 Your answers might be something like:

Brush my teeth, Get dressed, Eat breakfast, Put on my coat

Assembly, Maths, Sports, Lunch, Art, Home time

Get home, Homework, Dinner, TV, Reading, Bed time

Pages 64–65

1 a. bananas   **b.** apples

c. pineapples

2 Your answers might be something like:

a. The Twin Days Festival

b. UFO Congress Convention

c. The World Toilet Summit

Pages 68–69

1 a. illegal   **b.** incorrect

c. imperfect   **d.** irresponsible

e. invisible

Pages 70–71

1 a. antisocial   **b.** anticlimax

c. rethink   **d.** antigravity

e. reinventing

Pages 72–73

1 a. interact   **b.** autographs

c. interstellar   **d.** autopilot

e. intercity

Pages 74–75

1 Your answers should be something like:

a. a person who likes (or loves) books

b. a fear of spiders

c. speaking two languages

d. the study of stars

2 Your answers should be something like:

a. life   **b.** one or single   **c.** new

Pages 76–77

1 a. poisonous, harmful

b. cramped, small

c. healthy, nutritious

d. calm, peaceful

2 a. uneven, bumpy

b. tiny, minuscule

c. dangerous, harmful

3 Your answers might include some of these changes:

hard > difficult

hot > burning

tired > exhausted

hungry > starving

shiny > glistening

dry > parched
yummy > delicious

Pages 78–79

1 a. tasty **b.** miserable
c. enjoy **d.** easy

2 blunt – sharp
fear – courage
alone – together
beginning – end
artificial – natural
arrival – departure
maximum – minimum
innocent – guilty
near – far
ancient – modern
freezing – burning
bitter – sweet

Pages 82–85

1 a. aloud **b.** moose **c.** weather
d. peace **e.** genes **f.** night
g. heard **h.** flower

2 a. piece **b.** genes **c.** effect
d. banned **e.** except **f.** grown

3 a. jeans   **b.** flour

c. mousse   **d.** knight

e. moose   **f.** night

g. peace   **h.** flower

i. genes   **j.** piece

4 a. affect **b.** effect **c.** affect
d. effect **e.** affect **f.** effect

Pages 86–87

1 a. glasses **b.** duck
c. right **d.** spring

2 a. **b.** **c.**

d. **e.** **f.**

Pages 88–89

1 a. Wednesday
b. Yang
c. the Italian cheese
d. the thunderstorm
e. Oz
f. Bearnice

Pages 90–91

1 Synonyms: perfect, ideal, blissful
Word pairs: childhood, setting, countryside
Sentence example: Bearnice danced on the idyllic hillside.

2 Synonyms: healthy, luxurious, rich
Word pairs: garden, greenery, rainforest
Sentence example: The lush forest was full of life.

Pages 92–93

1 Synonyms: shocked, amazed, surprised
Word pairs: silence, expression, spectator
Sentence example: She was astonished to find out that aliens existed.

2 Synonyms: shocked, astonished, surprised
Word pairs: reaction, audience, onlooker
Sentence example: Shang High was totally flabbergasted when he won the lottery.

3 Synonyms: disbelieving, unconvinced, doubtful
Word pairs: stare, silence, reaction
Sentence example: Yang was incredulous as she stared at the monster.

4 Synonyms: dazed, stupefied, amazed
Word pairs: surprise, expression, silence
Sentence example: Yang felt stunned that Ying would do this to her.

Pages 94–95

1 Synonyms: blabbed, exclaimed, let slip
Word pairs: accidentally, suddenly, awkwardly
Sentence example: Plato blurted out the answer.

2 Synonyms: hummed, murmured, buzzed
Word pairs: monotonously, away, endlessly
Sentence example: Bogart droned on for at least twenty minutes.

3 Synonyms: whined, sniffled, moaned
Word pairs: feebly, sadly, softly
Sentence example: Grit whimpered quietly to himself.

4 Synonyms: shrieked, wailed, yelped
Word pairs: loudly, shrilly, excitedly
Sentence example: Brick squealed when he saw the tiny mouse.

Pages 96–97

1 a. elephant in the room
  b. two peas in a pod
  c. spill the beans
  d. on cloud nine
  e. a piece of cake

Pages 98–99

1 a. Everyone has their own view on what is beautiful.

b. If you start something early, you will have an advantage over others.
c. Regularly doing something is the best way for you to improve.
d. You should not form an opinion based on something's or someone's appearance.
e. You should never hurt someone, even if they have hurt you.
f. You should not count on something until it is certain.
g. You will make better decisions if you ask for advice.
h. You should not criticise a gift, even if you do not like it.

Pages 102–103

1 technology, character, chemical

2 c: **c**art
  ck: so**ck**
  k: unmista**k**able, snowfla**k**e, pran**k**
  ch: a**ch**e, an**ch**or, e**ch**o

3 a. anchor   **b.** prank
  c. snowflake   **d.** unmistakable
  e. ache   **f.** echoed

Pages 104–105

1 chandelier, machine, moustache

2 sh: wa**sh**
  ss: i**ss**ue, ti**ss**ue
  s: **s**ugar, **s**ure
  ch: para**ch**ute, non**ch**alant, **ch**ef, bro**ch**ure

3 a. brochure   **b.** parachute
  c. chef   **d.** issue
  e. sugar   **f.** nonchalant

Pages 106–107

1 g: be**g**in, shru**g**, bra**g**
  gg: jo**gg**ed, bi**gg**er, plu**gg**ed
  gue: catalo**gue**, lea**gue**, dialo**gue**, intri**gue**d, pla**gue**, monolo**gue**

2 a. plague **b.** league **c.** catalogue

3 a. dialogue **b.** plugged
c. intrigued **d.** shrug

Pages 108-109

1 a. uni**que** **b.** slee**k**
c. mysti**que** **d.** atta**ck**

2 c: **c**areful
ck: feedba**ck**, flo**ck**
k: spar**k**, oa**k**
que: grotes**que**, uni**que**, opa**que**, anti**que**

3 a. unique **b.** sleek **c.** opaque
d. antique **e.** oak **f.** grotesque

Pages 110-111

1 s: **s**andal, **s**ensitive, **s**ucculent
ss: a**ss**embly, ki**ss**
c: de**c**ent
sc: **sc**enic, **sc**ent, fa**sc**inating, mu**sc**le

2 a. scent **b.** sandal **c.** kiss **d.** muscle

3 a. sensitive **b.** fascinating
c. muscly **d.** assembly
e. succulent **f.** scenic

Pages 112-113

1 a. Armie forgot his lines **comically**.
b. Grit charged at the dragon **nobly**.
c. Shang High composed his latest song **frantically**.
d. Oz cried all afternoon **tragically**.
e. Yin picked the flowers **gently**.
f. Brick performed the experiment **meticulously**.

Pages 114-117

1 dripped, nodding, hopped, begging, jogging

2 a. trimming **b.** slamming **c.** jumping
d. seeking **e.** forgetting **f.** toasting

3 a. bigger, biggest
b. cheaper, cheapest
c. slimmer, slimmest
d. hotter, hottest
e. thinner, thinnest
f. younger, youngest

4 tipped, crowned, winner, regretted, listened, eating, cooking, hottest, sighed

5 Your answer might be something like: "Plato spent all afternoon flipping pancakes." or "This is the saddest part of the story."

Pages 118-119

1 adoration, donation, determination, preparation, sensation

Pages 120-121

1 a. joyous **b.** humorous
c. synonymous **d.** advantageous
e. rigorous

2 famous, courageous, dangerous, poisonous, vigorous

Pages 122-123

1 a. enclosure **b.** structure
c. departure **d.** pleasure
e. signature **f.** sculpture

2 enclosure, sculpture, structure, pleasure, signature, departure

Pages 124-125

1 a. lib**rar**y **b.** disas**tr**ous
c. exer**cise** **d.** me**dic**ine
e. res**taur**ant **f.** **reig**n
g. pota**toe**s **h.** w**eight**

2 a. disastrous **b.** restaurant
c. exercise **d.** weights
e. medicine **f.** library
g. reigned **h.** potatoes

Pages 128–135

1 **a.** False   **b.** True   **c.** False   **d.** False

2 **a.** 5   **b.** 3   **c.** 1   **d.** 4   **e.** 2

3 Labyrinth

4 intricate – complicated
anxious – worried
unfortunate – unlucky
appalling – very bad

5 **Your answer might be something like:**
"The illustration shows that Theseus is strong, handsome, vain and self-obsessed."

6 "everybody held their breath" – everybody waited nervously

"the crowd went wild" – the crowd were happy and made lots of noise

"the labyrinth always wins" – nobody ever escapes from the labyrinth

7 **Your answer might be something like:**
"I do not think Theseus understood Ariadne's plan because he had a confused look on his face."

8 **Your answer might be something like:**
"I think Ariadne rolls her eyes because Theseus takes the credit for her clever idea."

Pages 136–141

1 a, c, d

2 c

3 **Your answer might be something like:**
"We see a bead of sweat roll down Brick's forehead." or "Get back inside!"

4 **Your answer might be something like:**
"This scene is tense because Brick speaks *urgently*." or "This scene is suspenseful because we cannot understand what Captain Bearnice is saying."

5 **Your answer might be something like:**
"It is a cliffhanger because we do not know what happens to Captain Bearnice at the end of the scene."

Pages 142–147

1 **Your answer might be something like:**
"Lila campaigned to attend Bronze Oak Primary School." or "Lila campaigned for accessibility for visually impaired pupils."

2 **Your answer might be something like:**
"Because she bravely spoke out about a cause she believed in."

3 **Your answer might be something like:**
"Amblyopia is caused by one or both eyes being unable to build a strong link to the brain."

4 Her brother

5 The school's board of governors, headteacher and staff

6 The basic rights and freedoms all people are entitled to

7 Special Educational Needs

8 **Your answer might be something like:**
"Reversing a situation to be the opposite of what it usually is."

9 succeed, flourish

10 **Your answer might be something like:**
"Education is a human right so should be accessible for all."

Pages 148–153

1 **Your answer might be something like:**
"To record your dreams while you're asleep."

2 b

3 DAYDREAM IN VIDEO GAMES and ANIMATE YOUR AFTERNOON NAP

4 Oz

5 Whether you dream about dangerous dragons, detestable dentists or disco dancing... this product is for you!

6 **Your answer might be something like:** "Positive reviews: "It changed my life!" – Bearnice" or "Slogans: Where all your dreams come true"

7 **Your answer might be something like:** "The words "selling fast" made me think I needed to buy one before they all sold out."

8 **Your answer might be something like:** "SUPERGUM is superfun! A million of your favourite flavours (fruity, fresh, fiery and more!) all in one piece of gum."

Pages 154–159

1 unmanned aerial vehicle

2 Filmmakers, wildlife conservationists and farmers

3 **Your answer might be something like:** "Wildlife conservationists use them to observe the habits of an endangered species."

4 **Your answer might be something like:** "Staying in place in the air."

5 Fans

6 **a.** hover   **b.** descend   **c.** ascend

7 **Your answer might be something like:** "Heavier items have more gravitational force pulling them down so need more thrust to be carried by a drone."

Page 160

1 **Your answer might be something like:** "Woah! That lizard is as fast as a sports car." or "This stew tastes like muddy boots."

Page 161

1 **a.** It was messy.
  b. She knows lots of words.
  c. It has soft and white fur.
  d. It has ups and downs.

Pages 172–175

2 steped > stepped
they > They
funguses > fungi
gosts > ghosts
Bogarts > Bogart's
Follow I > Follow me
upstairs," > upstairs?"
his > him
replied "We > replied, "We
mystery Bearnice > mystery, Bearnice
determind > determined
Apprehensively Shang High >
Apprehensively, Shang High

COOKED UP BY MRS WORDSMITH'S CREATIVE TEAM

Pedagogy Lead
Eleni Savva

Writers
Tatiana Barnes
Amelia Mehra

Academic Advisor
Emma Madden

Creative Director
Lady San Pedro

Designers
Holly Jones
Jess Macadam
Evelyn Wandernoth
James Webb

Lead Designer
James Sales

Producer
Leon Welters

Artists
Brett Coulson
Phil Mamuyac
Aghnia Mardiyah
Nicolò Mereu
Daniel J Permutt

With characters by
Craig Kellman

No animals were harmed in the making of these illustrations.

Project Managers
Senior Editor Helen Murray
Senior Designer Anna Formanek
Project Editor Lisa Stock

Senior Production Editor Jennifer Murray
Production Editor Siu Yin Chan
Senior Production Controller Mary Slater
Publishing Director Mark Searle

First published in Great Britain in 2022 by
Dorling Kindersley Limited
A Penguin Random House Company
DK, One Embassy Gardens, 8 Viaduct Gardens,
London SW11 7BW

The authorised representative in the EEA is
Dorling Kindersley Verlag GmbH. Arnulfstr. 124,
80636 Munich, Germany.

10 9 8 7 6 5 4 3 2
002–328327–May/2022

A CIP catalogue record for this book
is available from the British Library.
ISBN 978-0-2415-5468-5

Printed in Malaysia

www.dk.com

mrswordsmith.com

For the curious

MIX
Paper | Supporting
responsible forestry
FSC™ C018179

This book was made with Forest
Stewardship Council™ certified
paper – one small step in DK's
commitment to a sustainable future.
Learn more at
www.dk.com/uk/information/sustainability

The building blocks of reading

READ TO LEARN

LEARN TO READ

| Phonemic Awareness | Phonics | Fluency | Vocabulary | Reading Comprehension |

Readiculous App
App Store & Google Play

Word Tag App
App Store & Google Play

OUR JOB IS TO INCREASE YOUR CHILD'S READING AGE

This book adheres to the science of reading. Our research-backed learning helps children progress through phonemic awareness, phonics, fluency, vocabulary and reading comprehension.